MAKING
DISCIPLES
IN YOUR
Community

COMING TOGETHER TO GROW IN CHRIST

A BIBLE STUDY BY
BARBARA HENRY

D1226078

Advancing the Ministries of the Gospel

AMG *Publishers*™

God's Word to you is our highest calling.

Following God

MAKING DISCIPLES IN YOUR COMMUNITY

Published by AMG Publishers. All Rights Reserved.

ISBN 10: 0-89957-346-0
ISBN 13: 978-089957-346-5

Cover design by ImageWright Marketing and Design, Chattanooga, TN
Layout by Rick Steele and Jennifer Ross
Editing by Rick Steele

Printed in Canada
14 13 12 11 10 09 –T– 7 6 5 4 3 2 1

This book is dedicated to my brothers and sisters in the Greenwood Community Group who with excellence, self-control, perseverance, and godliness have shared their faith, kindness, and love with me.

Acknowledgments

I would like to thank the following communities:

- Crosspoint Churches of Seattle, Washington

- The Gray's Parish group, the first community who helped me in the initial stages

- Covenant Theological Seminary and their gracious gifts to me as a visiting writer

- The various communities in St. Louis during the research phase: the communities at Orion and Craig House, my covenant community group at the seminary, the ladies from Grace and Peace, and the Captain's group

- The West Seattle Community group who worked with me to discover how Christ perfectly reflected each part of the divine nature

- The Mountlake Terrace Community group for their perseverance

- The Community of Grandmas and their desire for godliness

- Women in Prayer and their love

- My neighbors in Parkwood, who piloted an outreach version

- My critique group from the Northwest Christian Writer's Association, and Agnes Lawless who carefully edited the complete manuscript

- My faithful prayer partners

- The community at AMG Publishers

- My family, who are my most treasured community of faith

- Above all, the community of the Trinity

 In Him,

Barbara

About the Author

Barbara Henry has been involved in discipling ministries for over thirty years and led both faith community groups and neighborhood Bible studies. She received her B.A. in education from Covenant College and her M.A. in biblical counseling from Colorado Christian University, where she studied under Larry Crabb and Dan Allender. Currently, she is the Women's Chaplain at Crosspoint Green Lake Church in Seattle, Washington. Her passion for equipping others for ministry makes her a popular speaker in churches across America.

Barbara has four grown children who all love and serve the Lord. Her daughters, BJ and Sara, have given her seven grandchildren who love their Nana and bring her great delight. Her sons, Nathan and Daniel, are both pursuing careers in ministry. Additional information is available on her Web site,

www.barbarahenry.com

About the Following God Series

Three authors and fellow ministers, Wayne Barber, Eddie Rasnake, and Rick Shepherd, teamed up in 1998 to write a character-based Bible study for AMG Publishers. Their collaboration developed into the title, *Life Principles from the Old Testament.* Since 1998, these same authors and AMG Publishers have produced five more character-based studies—each consisting of twelve lessons geared around a five-day study of a particular Bible personality. More studies of this type are in the works. Over the years, more authors were acquired for the series, and new types of studies have since been published in an ongoing effort to add fresh perspectives as to what it means to follow God. However, the interactive study format that readers have come to love remains constant in all of our newest titles. As new Bible studies are being planned, our focus remains the same: to provide excellent Bible study materials that point people to God's Word in ways that allow them to apply truths to their own lives. More information on this groundbreaking series along with a free leader's guide for this study can be found on the following web page:

www.amgpublishers.com

Preface

Christianity stands alone because Christians stand together. It is the only religion based on relationships, and the way disciples are made reflects that distinction. Every other religion operates on the assumption that to be a good disciple one must try hard to please his god or gods, to maintain the disciplines set forth in sacred writings, and to master his own sinful cravings—each individual is on his own spiritual journey. Christianity is different. Our relationships with Christ and other believers enable us to grow together. Christ showed us the way to make disciples in community and His apostles wrote careful instructions on carrying out their Master's spiritual growth plan.

Since the reformation, a "personal relationship with Christ" has become the primary goal for many believers. We all understand the importance of that relationship, but with the modern emphasis on the individual, some have forgotten the importance of our relationships with each another. When this happens, we fail to see the riches and beauty of God's gifts to us that He wants us to find in one another.

The purpose of this study is to help you discover what Scripture says about discipleship. As the title suggests, I believe Scripture shows and tells us that making disciples is best done in community. Using the outline for spiritual growth given in 2 Peter 1:5–7 as a guide, we will explore other passages teach about making disciples. The first lesson focuses on Peter's experience and writing about discipleship. Each of the following lessons takes one quality Peter lists and studies one of the epistles that focuses on that quality. In addition, each lesson opens with a story of a successful community on the cutting edge of effective discipleship. These examples will give you discussion material and ideas to help your particular community improve its relationships and ministries.

I believe the whole community is called to disciple the whole community as each person contributes gifts and experiences he or she has been given. In a healthy community, all of us are released to use our gifts to build up the body of Christ in love. May the Lord use this study to help you and your community discover how He wants to use and bless you.

Following Christ,

Barbara Henry

Table of Contents

How to Use This Study

1. **Making disciples is primarily accomplished in community.** This study was developed for use in communities of faith that are dedicated to spiritual growth and mutual accountability.

2. **A personal desire for growth and for connection with others will provide stimulus for discipleship.** Personal preparation for group discussions will enhance your time together. And your time together will also enhance your personal growth. Relationships built in the context of a corporate pursuit of God will lead to deeper relationships with one another and with God.

3. **As a nine-week study, the daily readings are for personal use.** The community would not have time to do the Bible study together. Their discussions would focus on sharing what was discovered, giving time for confession, prayer, community building, and love.

4. **As a year-long study, a community would use one day's study for group discussion on a weekly basis.** The Bible study done in this way provides enough material for forty-five weeks or more.

5. **If your group has not met together prior to the beginning of the study, I suggest that you spend a few sessions together sharing your stories.** This is one of the best ways to get to know one another, but also to practice honest and open communication. It has a way of breaking down natural barriers and helping each person feel known and accepted

6. **Try to have access to a New American Standard Bible.** Most questions are based on the wording of this version. Other versions will often help you discover the full meaning of the passage, but the NASB will clarify the questions.

7. **Try not to read the author's comments before you study the passage for yourself.** The comments are not "the answers." Although I have put years of prayerful research into my comments, and they have been scrutinized by well-respected theologians, they are still just comments, and not intended to be the answer. The answers are found in the Bible and will be revealed by the Holy Spirit, so your main focus should be there. The questions are meant to help you discover what Scripture is saying and to promote discussion with others. What is happening in your own life and the life of your community will most likely be God's primary tool for applying His Word to you.

8. **For those who are involved in community outreach there will be ongoing conversations online (at www.barbarahenry.com) about how this study leads to exciting ways to share with your neighbors.** Once you have studied the passages and discussed them together

with your faith community, you may find both the concepts and the connections you have made provide a base for outreach. Some groups may choose to meet every other week with folks from their neighborhood to share insights and stories their studies have uncovered, in a relational, non-threatening environment. Nonbelievers may not be attracted to in-depth Bible study, but a discussion group focused on community building and loving care would be welcome to most people.

9. **Make prayer for your spiritual growth, for the making of disciples, and for the lost in your community a high priority.** Your personal study time will be most effective if it is bathed in prayer. Also, dedicate a good portion of your time together for corporate prayer. Prayer for one another and for the neighbors you seek to reach will be a vital part of your ministry.

1

Discipleship

Have you ever noticed that God's first words to Adam and Eve are significantly similar to Christ's last words to His disciples? God blessed Adam and Eve and said to them, *"Be fruitful and multiply."* Adam and Eve carried out God's directive by loving one another and forming a family. God used their coming together, their oneness, and their intimacy to create and nourish new life. Many centuries later, Christ blessed His first followers and said to them, *"Make disciples."* Making disciples is how we multiply. We are to carry out His directive similar to the way Adam and Eve did. Our coming together as His family, our oneness or unity as a community of Christ followers, and our honest and open transparency with one another creates and nourishes new spiritual life.

The process of spiritual birth is similar to physical birth. Conception, pregnancy, delivery, and growth correlate with seed planting, watering, conversion, and spiritual growth. Both processes are meant to happen in a loving environment, but in our fallen world many do not experience the ideal. Baby Christians are too often left on their own to try to figure out what the spiritual life is all about because making disciples is not seen as the high priority Christ gave it. Therefore, it is important that we study the Word of God to find the pattern the Lord has given us for making disciples and seek the guidance of His Holy Spirit to carry out His directions as closely as possible.

Word Study
MAKE DISCIPLES

A common New Testament Greek word for "disciple" is *mathetes*. It is a noun used 269 times in the New Testament to identify the followers of Christ. A verb form of the word, *matheteuoare,* is used in Matthew 28:19 and is found nowhere else in the Bible. It is an active word that means to make others into disciples. The church refers to this process as discipleship.

Stephen Smallman pastored a church in the Washington, D.C. area for forty years. He helped that church understand how we experience the new birth and trained its members to be spiritual midwives. He has recently published an excellent book called *Spiritual Birthline,*[1] which thoroughly develops the correlation between physical and spiritual birth. In this study, we will seek to take that same application to its next step. Making disciples involves both bringing people to conversion and nurturing them to full maturity. Our goal is to discover how God wants us to make disciples. We will seek to understand what He has already accomplished for us, what He desires to give us, and what He wants us to do.

INDIVIDUAL DISCIPLESHIP AND/OR COMMUNITY DISCIPLESHIP

For too long, we have seen spiritual growth as a private pursuit. The typical American evangelical often considers salvation only as a personal affair with Christ. We are taught that growth is an individual responsibility therefore we expect to become more like Christ by our own efforts. To keep things personal and private, discipleship develops into a mentoring model that limits insight and accountability to just one other person. We have lost the importance of community in the modern emphasis on individualism. Our sense of isolation has grown even more acute in the computer age. But in the postmodern culture we now find a growing desire for community and a realization of what we have lost in our isolation and pursuit of privacy.

This study seeks to take an in-depth look at how we grow spiritually in community. For our purposes, "community" is defined as a group of seekers or believers who come together regularly for mutual edification and encouragement, to study the Scriptures, to pray, and to share their faith in order to grow as disciples of Christ.

In his second letter to the early church, Peter gave his readers a list of qualities describing mature believers. Each lesson of this study focuses on **one** of the qualities, how we obtain it, how it grows in us, and how it relates to the others. This first lesson will explore the context of the verses that contain this list to help us understand what the qualities are and how to pursue them.

Before we look at 2 Peter 1, we will study several passages that describe Peter's experience of and teaching about discipleship.

📖 Read Matthew 28:19–20. What do you think Peter would have thought about Jesus' instruction to make disciples? How had Jesus discipled Peter?

_____

_____

_____

_____

_____

Word Study
COMMUNITY

A group of seekers or believers who come together regularly for mutual edification and encouragement, to study the Scriptures, to pray, and to share their faith in order to grow.

Dr. David Chapman, professor of New Testament at Covenant Theological Seminary teaches that the only imperative (direct command) in what we call the Great Commission is to *"make disciples."* The string of participles that surrounds this command describes how we make disciples. These participles function as adverbs in the Greek: *going, baptizing,* and *teaching.*[2] *Going* can involve travel to far distant countries or just across the street. We are to go to people, to their homes, to their cultures, to their circle of friends in order to make disciples. *Baptizing* is in the name of the Father, Son, and Spirit. This initiates them into fellowship with each member of the Trinity as well as into the fellowship of God's family. *Teaching* is described in terms of doing, observing, and obeying—implying actively walking in Christ's commands. This means walking alongside people, just as Jesus walked and taught His disciples, not in a classroom or individually but by living with and teaching them as a group.

APPLY   Is making disciples the primary goal in your church or community group? If not, what seems to be the primary goal now?

_____

_____

_____

What would need to change so our goals are the same as Christ's?

_____

_____

Read John 8:31–32; 13:34–35; and 15:8. How does Jesus describe true disciples? How do you think this would affect Peter's concept of making disciples?

_____

_____

_____

Jesus says true disciples abide in the Word, love one another, and bear fruit. He emphasized these in all His training of His disciples, and they, in turn, would have passed them to their disciples. As we make disciples, we also must teach them to observe the things that Christ commanded.

APPLY   Does your community group emphasize these three ideas? How much of your time together is spent in reading and studying God's Word? What do you do to build love for one another? What kind of fruit is produced?

_____

_____

_____

Read 1 Peter 2:1–5. How do disciples grow? How do the metaphors that Peter uses picture growth?

_____

_____

_____

"You also, as living stones, are being built up as a spiritual house for a holy priesthood."

1 Peter 2:5

Peter's first metaphor focuses on the individual Christian as a baby, longing for milk. The milk is the Word of God, and we grow as we feast on it. Peter's second metaphor focuses on corporate growth. He sees individuals as living stones that are connected to one another, being built into a spiritual house. Our growth must always include both individual and corporate growth. When it does, we become a holy priesthood, and together we offer spiritual sacrifices to God through Jesus Christ.

 What do you think it means that we are a holy priesthood? What does it mean to be a priest? What responsibilities does a priest have?

_____

_____

_____

_____

I explored this question when preparing to write a Bible study on Titus 2:3–5. The description of older women who are to train younger women literally means having lifestyles proper to priests. As I studied the lifestyle of the priests of the Old Testament, I found intriguing descriptions such as: being set apart for God, giving praise to God, praying, hearing confessions, assuring others of forgiveness, helping others connect with God, teaching the Word of God, sacrificing, and leading others in the ways of God.

What are some spiritual sacrifices we could offer to God?

_____

_____

_____

The gifts He has in store for you and your community are amazing. They are life changing and will enrich you in ways you never thought possible.

📖 Read 1 Peter 3:8–9. What do Peter's instructions in these verses add to our understanding about the purpose of our community groups? Why do you think the way we relate to one another affects our inheriting a blessing? What do you think is the blessing?

_____

_____

_____

I included these verses to whet your appetite for the blessing in store for you in this study. God is so good, and He wants to bless you beyond your fondest dreams. The gifts He has in store for you and your community are amazing. They are life changing and will enrich you in ways you never thought possible.

Discipleship

DAY TWO

GRANTS VS. HUMAN EFFORT IN DISCIPLESHIP

So much of individual discipleship is based on human effort and is fueled by self-discipline. However, if we look closely at our passage in 2 Peter, we will see that Peter describes discipleship or growth in our Christian lives in terms of grants, promises, partaking, and bringing in gifts to the community of faith. The wording in some translations of verse 5 suggests the importance of human effort and self-discipline, but as we consider possible alternate meaning of the Greek phrases, Peter's emphasis on God's grants and gifts will become clearer.

📖 Read 2 Peter 1:1–4. What is the origin of *faith* according to these verses? How are *grace* and *peace* multiplied to us?

_____

_____

_____

Peter declares that God imparts our faith to us through the righteousness of His Son, our savior, Jesus Christ. Paul in Ephesians 2:8 tells us faith is a gift of God. Grace and peace are also gifts that are multiplied in us as our knowledge of God the Father and His Son, Jesus grows.

📖 What do you think are the *precious promises,* and how are they granted to us? What is a grant?

_____

_____

_____

Surely faith, grace, and peace are among the precious promises granted to us through the true knowledge of God, but these verses tell us that everything we need for life and godliness are also included. A grant is a gift given for a particular purpose. The person who receives the grant is obligated to use it for its designated purpose. Verse 4 tells us the purpose of the grant is for us to become partakers of the divine nature. When we receive and live out of His precious promises, we partake of His nature, which lives and grows in a completely contrary manner to that of a corrupting world.

🛑 **APPLY** What do you think it means to partake of God's nature? Can you honestly say your deepest desire is to be like Jesus, having His nature in you?

_____

_____

_____

How willing are you to escape the corruption of the world? In what ways does it still have its hold on you? Are you still holding onto some part of it?

_____

_____

_____

_____

📖 Read 2 Peter 1:5. Notice verse five starts with *"For this reason."* In what way do you think that ties together the ideas listed before and after this phrase? How do God's promises and His divine nature relate to the list that begins in verse 5?

_____

_____

_____

"Seeing that His divine power has granted to us everything pertaining to life and godliness, through the true knowledge of Him who called us by His own glory and excellence, for by these He has granted to us His precious and magnificent promises."

2 Peter 1:3–4

Word Study
PARTAKERS

Partakers are those who share something in common, which leads to becoming companions, partners, or coworkers. *Webster's Dictionary* defines it as "1: to take a part or share, participate 2: to have some of the qualities or attributes of something."

Source: *Webster's Seventh New Collegiate Dictionary,* 614.

_____

_____

The King James (KJV) and New International (NIV) translations seem to imply a linear approach to spiritual growth. The implication is that faith is a gift and the rest of our growth is our responsibility. We *"add"* to our faith virtue, knowledge, etc. However, a closer look at the original Greek reveals this verse could actually be a list of the precious promises Peter refers to in verse 4. Rather than creating responsibilities of having to add to our faith, perhaps we are to appropriate these gifts. John Sanderson, a well-respected theologian of the twentieth century, offers the following illustration to help us picture Peter's metaphor:

> As a preliminary to grasping Peter's thought let me remind you of an experience many of us have had on such special occasions as anniversaries, birthdays, or going-away parties. At an appropriate moment someone presented the guest of honor with a large box, beautifully wrapped and tied with colorful ribbons. The guest pulled off the bow and removed the wrapping paper, and then opened the box. Inside that box was a somewhat smaller box similarly wrapped and adorned with ribbons. When those wrappings were removed, another boxed appeared and so on, box after box, until the guest arrived at a very small box which contained often a very valuable gift. That experience may help us understand Peter's point . . . The first box is "faith," the source of all blessings and fruit in the Christian life. Faith which has united us to Christ, which has laid hold on all the promises of God – that faith has in it all we need for life and godliness."

Rather than imagining a straight line where one thing is added to another, think of concentric circles or boxes as Sanderson suggests. It is helpful to realize the small word *"in"* is repeated seven times in the Greek, but is omitted by the King James and New International Versions. It is clear from the literal Greek that excellence is found *"in"* the faith, and that knowledge is *"in"* the excellence. Although it takes careful study to see this and understand its significance, it is important that we not omit the *"in"* or overlook Peter's reasons for putting it there.

APPLY If *"this reason"* mentioned in verse 5 is the wonderful fact that God is offering grants, promises, and His own nature for us to appropriate, how does that make you feel? Are you curious to open each gift and explore its significance in your life and community?

_____

_____

_____

Read 2 Peter 3:14–18. What is Peter's warning in this passage? Why is it important to apply it to this study, as well as to specific translations or interpretations of Scripture?

_____

_____

_____

I am fearful to suggest an interpretation of Scripture that seems different than the implications of accepted translations. Only after much prayer, and struggle, and discussions with Greek scholars do I suggest we look at the original text from a different angle, with open minds, and much care not to distort the Scriptures. Tomorrow we will attempt to tackle more of the original Greek phrases in verse 5 in an effort to explore possible meaning. Please join me in praying that none of us would be carried away by error. May we grow in the grace and knowledge of our Lord and Savior Jesus Christ.

 Why do you think the Bible is difficult to understand at times?

_____

_____

_____

Discipleship

DAY THREE

PARTAKING OF THE DIVINE NATURE TOGETHER

Since the beginning of time eating together has been a means of fellowship, celebration, and unity. In the Old Testament feasting together was very common. The children of Israel cemented covenants by eating together. Also, at the end of every peacemaking process, the participants would sit down to a meal together to express their unity. Likewise, in the New Testament eating was one of the most common things the church did together. Because it was an expression of unity, believers were told not to eat with a brother who refused to repent of his sins. The Lord's Supper uses the act of eating together to illustrate and celebrate our partaking of the divine nature together. Today, we will further explore what partaking of the divine nature means as we look closer at 2 Peter 1:5 and other related verses.

📖 Read 2 Peter 1:5 again. How do we *"apply all diligence?"* Do you think we do this alone or together?

_____

_____

_____

How we apply diligence depends on whether we are acting as individuals or as a group. In the Greek all the pronouns in this passage are plural. English does not have a distinct plural for "you" except in the southern United States. Try reading this verse with *y'all* substituted for *you*. Then consider the word, *apply*. The literal meaning in the Greek is "bringing in." This makes me want to ask, what do we bring in, where do we bring it, and why do we need to bring it in? Since the context is about grants, precious promises, and the divine nature, I suggest that is what we bring in. If what we bring in are the promises, *where* we bring it would be into our community. And *why* we need to bring the promises or gifts in would be to unwrap them together, and share them with each other, or partake of them together. Jesus said that when two or three of us are together, He is in our midst. When we come together, we bring Him in, and we also bring in the gifts He offers us.

The word diligence in this verse does imply responsibility, but the context indicates that we are responsible to bring in, in order to **partake** and not to produce something by our own efforts. It is important to discover what we need to be diligent about. If we diligently add these virtues to our lives by our own efforts, then we need self-discipline. If we diligently bring in the gifts Christ offers and partake of them together, we need to commit our time, our honesty, and our generosity to a community.

 Read 2 Peter 1:5 in the word-by-word translation from the Greek in the sidebar. The next phrase in our verse is literally translated *"supply in the faith of y'all."* What do you think this might mean? How would you explain the corporate nature of our faith?

_____

_____

_____

The word translated "supply" (NASB) or "add" (NIV) is *epichoregeo*. As a verb, it indicates an action, but it is important to see that we *supply* in our corporate faith. Let's look first at other uses of this word *supply*, and then focus on what it might mean to supply in our combined faith.

Epichoregeo is only used in four other places in the New Testament. The closest usage is in 2 Peter 1:11, an item we will look at a little later in our study of this passage. Second Corinthians 9:10 says, *"He who supplies [epichoregeo] seed to the sower . . . will supply [epichoregeo] and increase your righteousness."* Galatians 3:5 says, *"He who supplies [epichoregeo] the Spirit to you . . . by faith"* (ESV). Colossians 2:19 adds, *"Not holding fast to the head, from whom the entire body, being supplied [epichoregeo] and held together by the joints and ligaments, grows with a growth which is from God."* A similar word, *epichoregia* is used in Ephesians 4:16: *"From whom the whole body, being fitted and held together by that which every joint supplies [epichoregia], according to the proper working of each individual part, causes the growth of the body for the building up of itself in love."*

All these passages refer to a *supply* of nourishment for spiritual growth. The supply in two of the verses is related to our joints—either to the Spirit or to one another. Peter's metaphorical touch point here reminds me of another one we looked at earlier—his comparison in 1 Peter 2:5 of "living stones" connected to one another as a spiritual house. The connections give the supply. We *supply* as we come together, as we are joined, fitted, and held together, as we share our faith with one another. Our diligence should be focused on bringing in and supplying in our mutual faith.

APPLY What difference do you see between the New International and literal Greek translations of 2 Peter 1:5? How significant do you think this is?

_____

_____

_____

I see a significant difference between *"supply in the faith of y'all,"* (Literal Greek to colloquial English rendering) and *"add to your faith"* (NIV rendering). Think about it. If Peter meant to say *add,* he would have used the common word for *add*; if he meant it to be a personal pursuit, we would expect him to use singular pronouns. The use of the rare word *epichoregeo* gives us

"Also for this very thing [or reason] but diligence all bringing in supply in the faith of you [plural] the virtue, and in the virtue the knowledge...."

Source: Greek – English New Testament, (Washington D.C.: Christianity Today, 1975), 697.

something to think about, and leads us to consider the important question of how we could supply something in our combined or shared faith.

The rest of this study will be an exploration of the corporate nature of our faith. We will make every effort to bring in all the grants and precious promises, to grow in the true knowledge of Christ, by being fitted and held together by the work of the Holy Spirit among us.

📖 Read John 6:53–58, 63. What did Jesus mean when He said we must eat His flesh and drink His blood in order to live forever? How do we do that? Do you think it's the same as partaking of the divine nature?

_____

_____

_____

_____

When Peter writes that we are to be *"partakers of the divine nature,"* he may have had in mind what Jesus taught in John 6. Just as the disciples were confused by Jesus' teaching when He first spoke these words, many throughout the ages question what He meant by eating His flesh and drinking His blood. Of course, our participation in the Lord's Supper is one way we do this, but the Lord's Supper is a picture of a deeper reality. In John 6:63 Jesus explained that He was speaking of a spiritual reality, not just a physical activity.

APPLY What are some ways you have experienced the **spiritual reality** of eating His flesh and drinking His blood?

_____

_____

_____

📖 Read Mark 14:22–24. What does Jesus mean by calling the Lord's Supper a covenant? Do we completely fulfill a partaking of His covenant when we drink the cup and eat the bread? What more might it signify?

_____

_____

_____

_____

_____

Both baptism and the Lord's Supper are signs of the covenant. They both symbolize spiritual realities. The first is a washing away of our sins and induction into the covenant family of God, and the second is a continuous reminder of our covenant connection with Christ. Covenants were common in Old Testament times, and God used a familiar practice to illustrate His connection with His people. A covenant was a way individuals, families, and/or communities bound themselves together. Each member of the covenant would vow to be there for the others, to share resources, to protect each other, to bless one another. Marriage is the most common illustration of a covenant, when two people vow to love and cherish one another for the rest of their lives.

We will make every effort to bring in all the grants and precious promises, to grow in the true knowledge of Christ, by being fitted and held together by the work of the Holy Spirit among us.

The wedding ring is a symbol of the unity of a husband and wife. To say that wearing the ring is all there is to that unity is as ridiculous as thinking taking the wine and bread is all there is to partaking of God's nature. Many blessings, gifts, and responsibilities are part of our covenant love. Just as a husband and wife spend their whole married life exploring all the ramifications of their covenant of love, we can use this study to examine many of the facets of covenant love in our communities.

APPLY Do you see yourself in a covenant with Christ? Is your union with Him as real to you as marriage would be? What are some covenant blessings you have already received and enjoyed?

_____

_____

_____

_____

_____

"For if these quali-ties are yours and are increasing, they render you neither useless nor unfruit-ful in the true knowledge of our Lord Jesus Christ. For he who lacks these qualities is blind or short-sighted, having forgotten his purification from his former sins."

2 Peter 1:8–9

PRACTICE IN COMMUNITY

Today, as we continue to study the context of 2 Peter 1:5–7, we will set the stage for community discipleship. In Day Three we learned about *epichoregeo,* or *supply*, and that same word is used again in the verses we will look at today. Remember, we found that other uses of *"supply"* referred to nourishment for spiritual growth. The origin of the word, which those in the early church may have known, was in the Greek theater. Michael Green, a biblical scholar and commentator, explains:

> The word *epichoregein*, "add," is a fascinating one. It is a vivid metaphor drawn from the Athenian drama festivals, in which a rich individual, called the *choregos*, since he paid the expenses for the chorus, joined with the poet and the state in putting on the plays. This could be an expensive business, and yet *choregi* vied with one another in the generosity of their equipment and training of the choruses. Thus the word came to mean generous and costly co-operation.[4]

Peter identifies God as the ultimate *choregos* in 2 Peter 1:11. And, if we apply the metaphor to its use in verse 5, Peter is calling us all to generous and costly cooperation. In order to make disciples of everyone in our community, we must all supply the gifts we have been given to one another.

📖 Read 2 Peter 1:8–9. What are the results of having these *qualities* or gifts? Why is failure to have them a matter of blindness rather than disobedience? What does that indicate to you?

_____

_____

_____

_____

_____

The results are usefulness and fruitfulness. Notice that having these *qualities* or gifts make us useful and fruitful *"in the true knowledge of our Lord Jesus Christ."* Our fruitfulness can never be apart from our union with Him. Our efforts, self-discipline, or virtues that come from our own knowledge or energy won't add anything.

If these *qualities* were responsibilities, as is implied by the New International Version, not having or practicing them would be a sign of disobedience. It seems that if we don't *add* them to our faith, we are disobeying a command. However, a reference to blindness and shortsightedness indicates a failure to see and apprehend a gift or grant that has been provided for us.

Remembering our purification from former sins takes us back to the work of Christ in our conversion. Remembering the power of His work in us at that point in our lives helps us realize the power of His work in us now. We need His powerful supply for both life and godliness, or as the theologians say, for both salvation and sanctification.

APPLY What happens to you personally when you forget the work of Christ in your life? How does that affect the rest of your community?

_____

_____

_____

Why are we so often tempted to do things on our own?

_____

_____

_____

📖 Read 2 Peter 1:10–11. How do we *"practice these things,"* and why does Peter say that the way is *"abundantly supplied"* (epichoregeo) to us?

_____

_____

_____

I believe we *practice* using the gifts Peter listed in verses 5–7 in community with the rest of the body of Christ. We can't practice love or any of the other gifts by ourselves. We cannot love in a vacuum. We need brothers and sisters to show kindness to. We are to pursue excellence and knowledge together. The idea that we practice in community will be confirmed, as we find that most references to each of the gifts in other Scriptures places them squarely in the midst of community.

The second use of *epichoregeo* in the original Greek text of 2 Peter makes it clear that ultimately, God is the One who supplies (*epichoregeo*) entrance into the eternal kingdom, as well as, *"all we need for life and godliness."* Our efforts are not directed to adding anything to His perfect plan of salvation and purification, but rather towards knowing Him and receiving the abundant supply He offers, then bringing it into the community of faith. After we *practice His supply* in community, we can then take it to the world.

Did You Know?

NUANCES IN BIBLE TRANSLATION

If a word is not in the original Greek, but is needed in English to make more sense, Bible translators will insert words into the text but set them in italic type. In 2 Peter 1:8 the word "qualities" is in italics in the New American Standard Bible text, which indicates that the original Greek reads *"If these are yours. . ."* So, it does not actually identify the words in verses 5–7 as "qualities," and we could just as easily call them gifts or grants, since that is what is indicated by verses 3–4.

APPLY What are some ways you can think of that you and your community might practice these gifts together? (In essence, we will be focusing on this question for the remainder of this study, but you might find it interesting to compare what you write here with what you will discover as we progress.)

_____

_____

_____

_____

📖 Read Acts 2:42–47. What are some ways the early church practiced these gifts?

_____

_____

_____

Many communities have studied this passage and tried to duplicate the early church's practice. Some have done it successfully, and others have not. By listing all the practices of the early church, we can see how it illustrates the kind of community God can produce. But if we simply take their practice as a model and try to duplicate it without partaking of God's divine nature or appropriating all His gifts, we will fail miserably. Instead, we should seek to obtain God's supply rather than to legislate certain practices.

APPLY What experiences have you had in churches that tried to duplicate the practices of the early church? Did this succeed or fail?

_____

_____

_____

MINISTRY AND HUMILITY IN COMMUNITY

Knowing I was working on a study about community, a friend forwarded a newspaper article about a Christian community that some have branded as a cult. This brought up the importance of declaring from the outset of this study some things we must be careful about as we consider what faith communities are and should be.

The group described in the article had started out with good intentions, similar to the ones we are seeking to establish. They emphasized community, living with each other, and sharing life together. But their togetherness doctrine eventually became constant mutual oversight and a means of control. Manipulation and a chain of command developed, even though they taught about humility and tried to avoid overbearing leadership by denying any titles. One major warning sign surfaced when this group became closed to anyone on the outside rather than reaching out to others.

Just because Satan has successfully destroyed communities, this should not give us cause to avoid community. Rather, we need to be aware of the dangers and proactive in seeing and pointing out warning signs when folks get too close to the edge, or sidetracked from the purposes of community that God's Word outlines.

📖 Read 1 Peter 4:8. What does Peter identify as the highest priority for any community? What does it mean to cover a multitude of sins?

_____

_____

_____

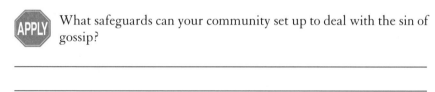

"Above all, keep fervent in your love for one another, because love covers a multitude of sins."

1 Peter 4:8

Love is the greatest and most important thing in our lives together. Love enables, protects, and maintains community. Without love communities would disintegrate. Love that covers sins provides not only the forgiveness and healing that comes with confessing our sins to one another, but also confidentiality.

An honest and transparent community should avoid gossip, or members will not be free to confess their sins. If you ever catch yourself or someone else talking about other's sins when they are not present, a big red light should go off in your head. It is a warning that Satan may be using you or others as his mouthpiece in his determination to accuse the brethren (see Revelation 12:10). We should be quick to identify the work of the enemy, and stand firm against him. We will also need to repent of our own sin of gossip.

 What safeguards can your community set up to deal with the sin of gossip?

_____

_____

_____

📖 Read 1 Peter 4:9. What is the next instruction Peter gives to communities? Why do you think he adds the phrase *"without complaint?"*

_____

_____

_____

The hospitality that Peter refers to has little in common with our culture's practice of entertaining. Rather, it is opening our homes and our lives to one another—first in our smaller community but eventually to the larger community and even to strangers. The *complaint* would most likely come from those who do not want to share, who resist generosity, or hold onto privacy. When we complain or feel resistance to the call to radical hospitality, we should see it as the exposure of root sins that need to be dealt with.

 What keeps a community from being self-focused and ingrown? How can we encourage one another to show more hospitality?

_____

_____

_____

_____

_____

_____

"As each one has received a special gift, employ it in serving one another, as good stewards of the manifold grace of God."

1 Peter 4:10

📖 Read 1 Peter 4:10–11. What is the third most important factor in a successful community? How is it to be carried out? Why?

_____

_____

_____

_____

Faith communities should guard against one gifted individual taking over and being the only one to use his or her gifts. Peter's blueprint for making disciples in community requires that all persons use their special gifts to serve the others. Being _"good stewards of the manifold grace of God"_ means we not only receive God's gifts of grace and use them to build up our communities, but we also make sure that everyone is encouraged to take part. Notice again Peter points out it is _"all done through Jesus Christ"_ so He will have the _"glory and dominion forever."_

APPLY What are some gifts people use in your community? How can you encourage others to use theirs as well?

_____

_____

_____

_____

📖 Read 1 Peter 5:1–4. What instructions does Peter give to the leadership? Why is this important? What happens when these instructions are ignored?

_____

_____

_____

_____

When leaders fail to serve and seek to control for their own gain and power, a community can turn into a cult. _"Lording it over"_ can manifest itself in a dictatorship that includes brainwashing and micromanagement. Power hungry individuals will use confessed sin as weapons of manipulation. Of course, it is not always that blatant or severe. The important thing to watch for is a growing measure of control. This can be a warning that the direction leaders are taking is dangerous. Oversight _"according to the will of God"_ is always gentle, voluntary, and exemplary.

APPLY Who do you think of as a good example of a godly leader? Describe him or her.

_____

_____

_____

📖 Read 1 Peter 5:5–7. Why is humility so important? What happens when pride takes over?

_____

_____

Notice that the members of the community must be humble toward one another. Whenever we fail to do this God will oppose us. That should scare the pride out of us, but pride is a squirrelly thing. It rushes in when we are not looking and establishes nests in our hearts. Our struggle against pride must be a constant battle. One warning sign that can help us identify pride is anxiety. Anxiety comes from a prideful heart that thinks it must care for itself. Humility comes from a heart that knows its poverty of spirit and its need of the Lord and His people for survival and growth.

APPLY What communities have you been a part of or heard of that have been damaged by pride and control? How did God oppose those people in leadership? What happened to the communities?

_____

_____

_____

_____

_____

What further safeguards can your community set up to deal with the sins of pride and control?

_____

_____

_____

At the end of each chapter we will include a sample prayer. But I encourage you to write one of your own in the space provided. It is a good way to review what you have studied, to pray through all the ways the Holy Spirit has spoken to your heart, and to confess sins He may have convicted you about. Also, be sure to take time in your group to "confess your sins to one another and pray for one another, so that you may be healed" (James 5:16).

_____

_____

_____

_____

_____

_____

_____

_____

_____

_____

"All of you, clothe yourselves with humility toward one another, for God is opposed to the proud, but gives grace to the humble."

1 Peter 5:5

Spend time with the Lord in prayer.

Father in Heaven, I thank and praise You for all You have provided for my life and godliness. I praise You that Your grace is sufficient for every need I have. I praise You, Christ, that You have freely given Your body and blood to establish a new covenant with Your people. I praise You, Holy Spirit, for applying to my heart the love of the Father, the grace of the Son, and Your own sweet presence. It will take an eternity to give You the worship You deserve for all You are and all You have done for us.

Lord, I confess my failure to keep "making disciples" a priority in my life. I have been too absorbed in my own private concerns and far too careless about Your kingdom. Christ told us to seek Your kingdom and Your righteousness first, but I have sought my own material gain and my own righteousness. Please forgive me, and change my heart to want what You want and to love what You love.

I confess, too, that I don't always want to partake of Your nature, and am too satisfied with my own. Sometimes I don't want to escape the corruption that is in the world and want to hold on to my lusts even though I know they can destroy me. O Father, please enable me to hate my sin, and to let go of the idols I still cling to. I especially want You to deal with my pride and control.

I pray You would enable our community to be one, to enjoy our unity, and to maintain peace. Please give us grace to be honest and transparent with one another and use that to create new spiritual life among us and nourish our spirits. Please help us to abide in Your Word, to love one another, and to bear fruit. Build us into a spiritual house that we might be a holy priesthood, giving You acceptable praise and honor.

Lord, deliver us from Satan's attempts to devour us and to destroy our community. Open our eyes to see what he is doing, and increase our faith to stand together—firm against him. Help us to see how our gossip is making us his mouthpiece. Reveal to us when our anxieties are nothing more than buying into his doubt and despair. Expose our pride and need to control as rebellion against Your sovereignty and loving care. Truly, Yours is the kingdom, and the power, and the glory forever—let us not seek any for ourselves.

Works Cited

1. Steven Smallman, *Spiritual Birthline* (Wheaton, IL: Crossway Books, 2006).

2. David W. Chapman, "The Great Commission as the Conclusion of Matthew's Gospel," in Robert A. Peterson and Sean M. Lucas, eds., *All For Jesus. A Celebration of the 50th Anniversary of Covenant Theological Seminary* (Fearne, Scotland: Mentor, 2006), 90.

3. John Sanderson, *The Fruit of the Spirit* (Phillipsburg, NJ: P and R Publishing, 1985), 143-146.

4. Michael Green, *The Tyndale New Testament Commentaries, The Second Epistle General of Peter* (Grand Rapids, MI: Eerdmans, 1968), 67.

2

Faith

*I*f you want to read an amazing story of the development of a community of faith, get a copy of Edith Schaeffer's book, *L'Abri*. Tucked away in a remote village on a mountainside in the Swiss Alps, you will find a number of chalets with open doors ready to provide shelter to strangers searching for truth and faith. My neighbor, Fiona, grew up there and remembers the excitement and joy of sharing their lives with many who came to visit. She recently returned as an adult and was most impressed with the living examples of faith and hospitality.

The love, joy, and peace of those who live by faith is very inviting. Another visitor said, "Everybody here at L'Abri seems to get a lot of joy simply out of living and being human. I've never seen anything like it before. I always imagined Christians would be narrow, depressed, and boring people. Yet I come here and find that you throw yourselves into life. You seem to understand how to live it."[1]

From the beginning of their ministry Francis and Edith Schaeffer, and all of those who have worked there, have adhered to L'Abri's purpose:

> To show forth by demonstration in our life and work the existence of God . . . to live on the basis of prayer in several realms:
>
> 1. We make our financial and material needs known to God alone.

L'Abri . . .

. . . a community of faith

"Faith is the attitude whereby a man abandons all reliance in his own efforts to obtain salvation [*and sanctification*], be they deeds of piety, of ethical goodness, or anything else. It is the attitude of complete trust in Christ, of reliance on Him alone for" [*life and godliness*].

Faith is reaching out to receive God's grace in Christ. Community faith is reaching out together.

Source: L. L. Morris, *The New Bible Dictionary* (Grand Rapids, MI: Eerdmans Publishing Co., 1976), 411.

Faith

DAY ONE

2 PETER 1:3–7

"Seeing that His divine power has granted to us everything we need for life and godliness . . . that you might become partakers of the divine nature. . . . For this reason bringing in with diligence supply in the **faith** *of y'all the excellence and in excellence the knowledge and in knowledge the self-control and in self-control the perseverance and in perseverance the godliness and in godliness the brotherly kindness and in brotherly kindness the love."*

(Author's Composite Translation)

2. We pray that God will bring the people of His choice to us, and keep all others away.
3. We pray that God will plan the work, and unfold His plan to us.
4. We pray that God will send the workers of His choice to us.[2]

This purpose is lived out in front of all the visitors and workers alike. Visitors are expected to work alongside those who live there, but everyone also has time for study and discussion. Every Monday they hold a community meeting and pray together for all their needs. Strangers and those not yet believers can watch and see their faith. They can experience the amazing answers to prayer as God provides everything they need and brings the people of His choice to them. Their dependence on God alone, the living demonstration of His trustworthiness, along with a clear presentation of truth have brought many to faith.

I believe the key to L'Abri is that those who live and work there have faith enough to live it out in front of others. The Schaeffers opened their lives and their home to share their faith. Isn't that what we are all called to do? They did not see faith as personal and private belief. Rather, they understood faith to be the basis of their life and community. Both evangelism and discipleship are carried out by living example, not just theoretical information. Communities that desire to teach and live out their faith together can learn much from the example of L'Abri. If we had more communities like theirs it would be easier to *"supply in our faith"* all the precious promises of God.

FAITH IN CHRIST

Normally on the first day of each lesson in this study, we will look at how Christ perfectly reflected the divine nature while He was here on earth. However, we will part from our normal pattern today and explore how we must be "in Christ" in order to partake of the divine nature. Faith is how we partake. The other qualities like excellence and knowledge are the gifts we are given as we share our faith.

Discipleship begins with faith and is completed in faith. Remember Sanderson's illustration used in the first chapter? He described faith as the big box where we will find and receive all the precious promises of God. Or we can think of it as the circle of faith which contains every grant God has provided for our life and godliness. Because of this, it is vitally important that we explore the meaning and basis of faith in order to grow in our faith.

📖 Read Ephesians 1:1–14. How many times does Paul use the word "in"? What do you think might be the significance of this small word?

_____

_____

_____

The most common prepositional phrase in this passage is *"in Christ."* Paul is emphasizing the truth that only those who are in Christ are faithful (verse 1) and have faith (verse 15). You are a Christian because you are in Christ and He is in you. This is the basis of faith.

The bedrock of faith is union. We long for union because we are made in God's image. Jesus prayed we would be in Him just as the Father was in Him and He was in the Father: *"even as Thou, Father, art in Me, and I in Thee, that they also may be in Us"* (John 17:21). Through verses like this one, we know there is unity in the Trinity. How amazing that Jesus is praying for a similar unity between us and God! And then He goes on to ask that the unity would extend to our relationships with each other: *"And the glory which Thou hast given Me I have given to them, that they may be one, just as We are one"* (John 17:22).

Think of all the pictures of union we have been given. God has given us examples like marriage, the family, and the church to help us realize the importance of unity. Romans 6:4–5 tells us baptism is a picture of union, and the Lord's Supper also reminds us of our union with Him. Partaking of His divine nature is accomplished in union and communion.

📖 Read Ephesians 1:3–6. Where does faith originate? What does it mean to be chosen in Christ? Are we chosen to be given faith, or are we in Christ because we have chosen faith?

_____

_____

_____

_____

It is important to see what Paul is saying about the origin of faith. Paul's description of how it happens reveals God as the active One, and we are the receivers. He blessed us, chose us, predestined us, adopted us, and bestowed grace on us—all in and through Christ. This was done according to the kind intention of His will, not because of what we do or say, or whatever faith we can muster. In this way He gets all the praise and glory.

 Would you agree that many in the visible church think they have faith because they understand faith to be their own choice to believe certain facts? How does lacking a vital union with Christ call into question the reality of their faith?

_____

_____

_____

📖 Read Ephesians 1:7–10. What benefits does faith bring according to these verses?

_____

_____

_____

With faith come redemption, forgiveness, grace, wisdom, and insight. We learned in the first chapter that in our corporate faith we supply excellence,

"I do not ask in behalf of these alone, but for those also who believe in Me through their word; that they may all be one; even as Thou, Father, art in Me, and I in Thee, that they also may be in Us."

John 17:20–21

knowledge, self-control, perseverance, godliness, brotherly kindness, and love. They are all found in Christ. We must partake of Him in order to partake of these gifts. But remember, we supply them in our faith. Faith brings them in to our community and practice. By faith we receive, partake, practice, and enjoy all the grants and gifts His grace supplies.

📖 Read Ephesians 1:11–14. What keeps our faith alive?

_____

_____

_____

If we focus on our own ability to keep our faith, we sink as surely as Peter did when he tried to walk on water and took his eyes off Christ (Matthew 14:30). Rather, we need to focus on Christ and receive all that He offers. This passage mentions three strong supports for our faith: our inheritance, the message of truth, and the Holy Spirit.

In some measure we have already obtained the first support for our faith—our inheritance. It is ours because God has predestined it for His own purposes. If our eternal security rested on our own abilities to keep the faith, we would be a sorry lot. Our hope is in Christ alone. Because He has done all that is needed to secure our inheritance, our faith rests in Him.

The message of truth or the gospel of our salvation is the second support for our faith. In essence, it is Word of God that brings us into faith and enables us to grow in faith. Again, John Sanderson explains it well:

> The word of God is the vehicle by which faith comes to us. This faith unites us to Christ who then justifies and sanctifies us and these acts of His are the source of our power. . . . Faith as sight enables us to see God's hand in everything, hence by faith we see the opportunities which provide for the exercise and development of our God-given character.[3]

Our faith grows in the Word. The more we hear and study the Word, the stronger our faith becomes.

And finally, the Holy Spirit seals and supports our faith. As a seal He marks us as God's own possession. His presence and work in us proves to our own spirits that we belong to Him, and the fruit He produces within us reveals to the rest of the world that we belong to Him. He is described in verse 14 as the pledge of our inheritance. This amazing union of His Spirit with our spirits is the down payment of the glorious wedding and communion that is to come.

APPLY   Has this study of Ephesians 1 increased your faith and sense of security or has it caused you to question the reality of your faith? Why or why not?

_____

_____

_____

_____

CHANGES FAITH BRINGS

Faith isn't just a ticket to heaven. Nor is it primarily a way to make our lives more enjoyable. Miroslav Volf in his excellent book *Free of Charge* says, "Faith is an expression of the fact that we exist so that the infinite God can dwell in us and work through us for the well-being of the whole creation."[4] He goes on to explain that the gift of faith not only deals with our guilt, but also makes major changes in our lives:

> God doesn't just forgive sin; He transforms sinners into Christ-like figures and clothes them with Christ's righteousness. . . . Intimate communion with God has been God's goal with humanity from the beginning. We are made for God to live in us and for us to live in God.

As we will see in the study of Ephesians 2, this communion is not only with God but also with the children of God.

📖 Read Ephesians 2:1–3. What were the Ephesians like before they had faith? What does it mean to be children of wrath by nature?

_____

_____

_____

Since the Fall in the Garden of Eden, Adam and Eve and all their children have been dead in sins. All of us were born under the power and influence of the evil one. We are not as independent and self-ruled as we thought. By nature we are all sons of disobedience. Because we are children of Adam and Eve, we are also children of wrath—under the wrath of God. Without faith we are slaves to our fleshly passions and thoughts.

APPLY Do you remember when you were dead in your sins? How would you explain to an unbeliever the difference between your former deadness and what it is like to now be alive together with Christ?

_____

_____

_____

📖 Read Ephesians 2:4–10. What things had to happen to bring the Ephesians to faith?

_____

_____

_____

_____

I love the phrase *"But God!"* To be dead in sins is utterly hopeless. We can do nothing about our situations. *But God* can, and did. He had to act first. Because of His love and mercy, He made us alive with Christ. Because of His grace, He gave us faith. We are His workmanship. Whatever good works we do, they grow out of the faith He has given us, and are accomplished by His grace. He gets all the glory.

I love the phrase "But God!"

The phrase in verse 6, *"seated us with Him in the heavenly places"* may be a bit confusing for some. If we think of it in relation to his description in verse 2 of *"the prince of the power of the air"* we see that God has placed us in Christ above the powers that used to control us. In Christ we are seated in a place of authority where the enemy of our souls cannot reach us. We can now say to Satan, "You no longer have any authority in my life."

APPLY How does realizing you are God's workmanship change the way you think about good works?

_____

_____

_____

God is the One who is doing the work. If we know that He prepares the works, gives us grace to do the works, and works through us, we are thankful that He would use us, instead of proud of what we do. We are not the primary source of good works, but these works are the result of God's work in us.

How would this change the way you do good works?

_____

_____

_____

We depend on Him more in the midst of our work. Prayer becomes our primary responsibility. We are looking to Him to guide us, to enable us, to work in us and through us. Apart from Him we can do nothing (John 15:5).

📖 Read Ephesians 2:11–12. What are hopeless people missing? What three things has God provided to give us hope? How might each of them help us when we feel a lack of faith?

_____

_____

_____

_____

We lose hope when our rebelliousness separates us from Christ. We lose hope when we alienate ourselves from the fellowship of the saints (which in the New Testament takes the place of the commonwealth of Israel). We lose hope when we fail to hold on to the covenant of promise. God has given us Christ, the church, and His promises so that we might know Him and have hope. When we ignore these gifts, our faith diminishes, and we get depressed. When we focus on them and intentionally pursue them, we find our faith and our hope growing.

APPLY Next time you are pulled down into the mire of depression what will you do to regain hope?

_____

_____

_____

Whenever I feel depressed, I try to determine which of Christ's gifts I have ignored. If I am not truly following Him and have wandered off onto my own path, I need to repent and turn back to Him. If I have isolated myself from my community of faith, I need to initiate contact and pursue the relationships I have avoided. If I am having trouble believing the promises of God, I need to pray for increased faith, and ask my brothers and sisters to also pray for me.

📖 Read Ephesians 2:13–16. What major change did faith produce in the Ephesians? What laws were abolished by Christ's work on the cross? What are the extended implications?

_____

_____

_____

_____

The major change Paul deals with in this passage is that separation and alienation became inclusion because of Christ's work on the cross. He established peace and reconciliation. Oneness is now possible because of a shared faith. Paul finishes this chapter by saying that all those who have the gift of faith are fellow citizens with the saints and members of the household of God. We are joined together and are being built together. Our community becomes a dwelling place for God.

APPLY Towards whom in your faith community do you feel any alienation? How does realizing the reconciliation Christ accomplished on the cross break down any of the dividing walls that may exist?

_____

_____

_____

What reasons do you have to live in harmony with other believers in your community?

_____

_____

_____

Put Yourself in Their Shoes
DEPRESSION

Imagine you are sitting with someone who is struggling with depression. What questions would be appropriate to ask them?

❑ *Have you seen a doctor to find out if your depression may have a chemical component?*

❑ *What situations are you going through that may affect your feelings?*

❑ *In what ways are you being tempted to rebel against God?*

❑ *Are you meeting regularly with your community group?*

❑ *In what ways do you seek to remind yourself of God's covenant promises to you?*

❑ *Of what do you need to repent?*

❑ *How is your prayer life?*

(In most cases, all of the sample questions would be appropriate.)

THE PURPOSE OF FAITH

Faith

DAY THREE

For years I thought the purpose of faith was to connect me to God. My faith was a private affair. By personality I am an introvert, so this worked well for me. It also fit with my culture—independence and individuality were the cornerstones of my existence. But once the Lord gave me the corrective lenses of community, my vision of what Scripture has to say about faith has changed significantly. As you study the following passages in Ephesians, reconsider with me the purpose of faith. I believe we will find it not only has to do with our connection to God, but also our responsibility toward others, our appreciation for what others can offer us, and the full realization of the many facets of God's love that we can comprehend when we share our faith with others.

📖 Read Ephesians 1:15–19. What are the implied purposes of faith according to Paul's prayer? What three things does Paul specifically pray that the Ephesians would know in verses 18 and 19? What do you think they mean?

_____

_____

_____

_____

Without faith it is impossible to know God, His calling, His riches, or His power. God gives us faith so the eyes of our hearts will be open to all that He has for us. Since we are focusing on community in this study, I want to zero in on the phrase *"the riches of the glory of His inheritance in the saints."* This can be a rather confusing phrase, but starting at the end and working backwards will help us understand it. *The saints* are Christ's *inheritance* (see Ephesians 5:29 and Revelations 21:2). In other words, one day God the Father will give His Son His inheritance—the purified bride made up of all the saints. In the meantime, God is giving the saints a glory that will not only bless Christ, but we too will be blessed by knowing its riches. In other words, the *glory* He has given us (the saints) contains *riches* that are worth knowing. Paul prays that the Ephesians would know those riches, that they would see in others in their community what God wants to give them by the glory He has invested in each saint. By faith we look for those riches and expect to find them. The glory of Christ in every saint who belongs to our community can enrich us.

 What riches of the glory of the saints have you discovered and known? How have they enriched your life?

_____

_____

_____

In one of my community groups our leader had an amazing mind and often gave us the gift of knowledge. Another member had the gift of mercy and would grace us all with the kind of love and care Jesus gave others. One woman who was mentally challenged offered us wonderful riches in sharing some things Jesus had told her in her private times with Him. The glory in each individual was Christ in them. As each one shared the riches of the glory Christ gave them, we were all enriched.

📖 Read Ephesians 3:1–6, 10–12. What insight was Paul given regarding the mystery of Christ? What three specific details does he give in verse 6? What do they have to do with community and partaking of the divine nature? What is the purpose of faith according to verses 10–12?

_____

_____

"I pray that the eyes of your heart may be enlightened, so that you may know what is the hope of His calling, what are the riches . . . in the saints, and what is the surpassing greatness of His power toward us."

Ephesians 1:18–19

_____

_____

_____

From our study of Ephesians 2 we know Paul deals with the mystery of how the Gentiles are included in the gospel offer. Paul's focus is on the unity of believers, both Jews and Gentiles. He calls them fellow heirs, fellow members of the body, and fellow partakers of the promise. Please don't miss the corporate nature of being in Christ. God's manifold wisdom is made known through a united church. The purpose of the church is to make known this wisdom by our unity, by sharing the riches of His glory, by bringing to light the truth of the gospel. Faith in Christ gives us boldness and confident access to God, to His wisdom, and to one another.

 How would you summarize the purpose of faith after studying these passages? How does it change your view of Christ, the gospel, and the church?

_____

_____

_____

_____

As we gather together in our community groups, we each "bring in" our gift of faith, and then as we unwrap the gift before believers and unbelievers in our midst, we share our faith with one another. We do this by studying the Word together, honestly sharing who we are and how we seek to live by faith, and then praying with faith for all our needs. The purpose of faith is to unite our hearts together, to break down barriers, and to give us access to one another and ultimately to God. Think of all the barriers that were set up in the Garden of Eden after the Fall. Faith can break them all down and give us boldness and confident access once again.

📖 Read Ephesians 3:14–19. What do you think is the subject of the *"breadth, length, height, and depth"* in verse 18? What does it mean to comprehend it *"with all the saints?"* How does the plural "you" in verse 19 change Paul's image for you?

_____

_____

_____

This is an amazing prayer and one that we should pray often for ourselves and for one another. The phrase *"according to the riches of His glory"* reminds me of his prayer request in Ephesians 1:18. Remember we discovered that these riches are found in the saints. Every family is blessed with these riches in their unity and community. The Holy Spirit must strengthen us with power in our inner spirits so that Christ may dwell in our hearts through faith. This will ground us in love. The *breadth, length, height, and depth* must refer to love, since it is mentioned both before and after the phrase. I believe it is both the love of Christ that surpasses knowledge and the love we experience in the body of Christ. The fullness of God referred to in verse 19 is

> **The purpose of the church is to make known the manifold wisdom of God by our unity, by sharing the riches of His glory, by bringing to light the truth of the gospel.**

the same fullness he mentions in Ephesians 1:23 where he makes it clear he is talking about the body, or the church. God's fullness fills us corporately for the purpose of bringing glory to Christ in the church. All this is accomplished in us both individually and corporately by faith.

APPLY What is it going to take for you to know the *breadth, length, height, and depth* of love? How will your relationship to your community help?

_____

_____

_____

Have you ever experienced being *"filled up with all the fullness of God?"* What do you think that means? Do you think you can experience it alone?

_____

_____

_____

_____

THE GROWTH OF FAITH

Have you ever thought that your personal faith grows primarily by your effort to maintain spiritual disciplines? In all my thinking about this book, the question of what part the spiritual disciplines play in our growth continues to be most troubling to me. The answer has radical implications for the way we do discipleship. I can see how the idea of trying to be disciplined may have developed from the King James' translation of 2 Peter 1:5–7. If we are to make every effort to add to our faith a list of responsibilities that will come only by consistent discipline, we'd better get busy and stay busy. We will need to keep many rules to maintain our virtue, and read books to gain knowledge, and to check into a monastery to be sure we are totally devoted to God. But Ephesians 4 describes a different lifestyle. There we discover again that our growth is accomplished through partaking of God's divine nature in a shared faith.

📖 Read Ephesians 4:1–3. What is the *"unity of the Spirit"* and how do you think we maintain it?

_____

_____

_____

Did you notice that walking *"in a manner worthy of our calling"* has little to do with personal disciplines and everything to do with how we treat one another in our community life? Humility, gentleness, patience, and bearing with one another in love describe how we relate to others, not so much how we pursue personal holiness. Unity seems more important than personal and private piety. I believe preserving the unity of the Spirit has more to do with community and peace within the body of believers than a personal feeling of peace and well-being.

 In what ways do you preserve the unity of the Spirit in your community of faith?

_____

_____

_____

I am tempted to just keep quiet, and not make any waves. But I think that only preserves a false peace. If I am to help preserve the unity of the Spirit, I must at times confront sin and even differences, but with humility, gentleness, and patience. Longsuffering may take time and energy, but it is worth it.

📖 Read Ephesians 4:4–6. What do you think is Paul's point in listing all the ways we are one? Why is oneness important to our faith?

_____

_____

_____

Our bond of peace within a faith community is based on seven shared realities. Each of them connects us to one another in bonds that cannot be broken. Think of ways your faith grows because of the truth of each of the following realities:
- One body
- One Spirit
- One hope
- One Lord
- One faith
- One baptism
- One God and Father

 Which "one" reality has been meaningful to you recently? How has it built up your faith and the faith of those in your community?

_____

_____

_____

📖 Read Ephesians 4:11–14. How does our faith grow according to these verses?

_____

_____

_____

Verse 13 tells us that we reach maturity by *"attaining the unity of the faith and of the knowledge of the Son of God."* Unity of the faith does not refer to our holding identical views on specific doctrines—especially the controversial ones that Scripture is unclear about. Rather, unity of the faith refers to

"I entreat you to walk in a manner worthy of the calling with which you have been called, with all humility and gentleness, with patience, showing forbearance to one another in love."

Ephesians 4:1–2

 **Doctrine**
TESTED OR TEMPTED?

Being tested by God is different from being tempted. God doesn't tempt us (James 1:13); Satan does (Luke 4:1–2). However, God will use both our tests (trials and hardships) and temptations to strengthen us toward deeper dependence on and devotion to Himself. Like a muscle strengthened by the exertion we place on it, our faith is proved genuine by the exertion God places on it or allows to be placed on it. It is then strong enough and ready for the next test or temptation. A faith-bathed response to our tests and temptations not only proves our faith genuine, but our God faithful to those who are watching.

relationships that grow out of sharing faith and knowing the same Lord. The fullness of Christ is experienced as each of us uses our gifts to build up the body of Christ.

 What is your church doing to make disciples? How might a more direct application of these verses change that?

_____

_____

_____

 Read Ephesians 4:15–16. What are we building in the church, and how do we do it according to these verses?

_____

_____

_____

Verse 16 makes it clear that we are building love. The body is fitted and held together by the joints or connections our oneness provides. Every connection is a joint where love passes from one person to another. And the proper working of each individual part causes growth in faith for all of us. We are to speak the truth in love and build love, and that would be impossible to do alone.

Read the quote in the sidebar from *Thoughts on Religious Experience* by Archibald Alexander, a writer in the early seventeenth century. I would add to his thoughts that deriving our lives entirely from Christ involves partaking of His divine nature within the shared faith of a body of believers.

 What are some ways we get sidetracked in our building other things rather than love in our churches?

_____

_____

If spiritual disciplines are not the primary ways we grow spiritually, what is? How do you think the disciplines fit in?

_____

_____

_____

Faith

DAY FIVE

THE COMMUNITY OF FAITH

Robert Webber released his thought-provoking book, *Ancient-Future Evangelism*, in 2003. In it he explores how the ancient church engaged in evangelism and discipleship, and then he challenges today's church to factor in ancient practices into our future plans.

The subtitle of the book is *Making Your Church a Faith-Forming Community*. God used much of what he wrote to change my thinking about discipleship and put me on the road to writing this study.

> The church is not a perfect society, but it is God's society. . . . The new disciple must be immersed in the life of the church because it is the presence of God's life in the world. . . . In the postmodern world a new understanding of how learning takes place has emerged. It is learning through submersion in a culture. . . . When a new disciple is submerged in the communal life of the church—in its story, its values, its perspective—the countercultural nature of the faith is caught and the disciple begins to be formed by immersion in the ways of the community. [6]

📖 Read Ephesians 4:17–20. How do we *"learn Christ"* together? What do you think it means to *"walk in the futility of our minds?"* Why is that more likely when we are separated from community?

_____

_____

_____

_____

It is interesting to take each description that Paul gives of those who walk in the futility of their minds and think of the opposite, then imagine how a true community of believers would facilitate it. *"Darkened in their understanding"* would be replaced with the enlightenment of shared faith. *"Excluded from the life of God"* would be replaced with inclusion in the family of God. *"Ignorance"* would be replaced with shared knowledge and *"hardness of heart"* would be challenged by accountability. *"Callousness"* would become sensitivity, and *"sensuality"* would be replaced by spirituality. A true community practices purity and generosity rather than *"impurity"* and *"greediness."* Webber adds:

> We encounter Jesus through the church as it embodies truth. Conversion is not merely embracing an intellectual idea; it is taking one's place within the body of people who confess Christ and seek to live out the kingdom of Jesus. Thus one does not merely know intellectually but one knows holistically in community. [7]

APPLY Is your church a faith-forming community? What is its communal life like?

_____

_____

_____

What is God calling you to do to increase its effectiveness?

_____

_____

_____

Personally, I believe God has called me to write this study, but also to be more honest and transparent with my own community group. The first is easier than the second. The anonymity of writing seems safer than self-disclosure in a community.

> *"Walk no longer just as the Gentiles also walk, in the futility of their mind. . . . But you did not learn Christ in this way."*
>
> *Ephesians 4:17, 20*

📖 Read Ephesians 4:20–25. Where would the Ephesians have learned Christ, where would they have *"heard Him,"* and where were they *"taught in Him"*? How would they have learned what it meant to put off their old selves and be renewed in the spirit of their minds? What does being *" members of one another"* have to do with community? What reasons for speaking truth to one another are given in this passage ?

_____

_____

_____

_____

_____

The *"therefore"* in verse 25 ties the previous verses together with the idea of community. If we start at the end of verse 25 and work backwards, we see that because we are members of one another, we speak truth to one another. That renews our minds, and helps us lay aside our former manner of life. We *"learn Christ"* by being among those who are living in Him. We hear Him by hearing what He says through His Word, the truth spoken by Christ Himself or the apostles. We can even hear Him when our neighbors speak the truth.

APPLY What does being *"members of one another"* look like in your community? What are the best opportunities you have for speaking the truth to one another?

_____

_____

_____

Did You Know?

ACCUSER OF THE BRETHERN

One of the bestsellers of all time is the book, *The Screwtape Letters*. In this book, C.S. Lewis captures the truth of how the accuser of the brethren works in this imagined correspondence between Satan and his underling, Wormwood. Page after page, we see how he spreads his lies, accuses other believers, and tempts people to silence, to gossip, to selfishness, and sin.

📖 Read Ephesians 4:26–29. How does Satan try to break up community? What can we do to be sure he fails? How do anger, slothfulness, and gossip affect community?

_____

_____

_____

When we let the sun go down on our anger and don't speak the truth about it to the one who has offended us, we give Satan an opportunity to do his thing. As the accuser of the brethren, he puts false accusations in our minds, builds walls of division, and encourages selfishness, greed, and gossip. The phrase taken from Ephesians 4:15, *"speaking the truth in love,"* is our strongest weapon against him. Communication is one of the most important pillars of community. I believe the falsehood Paul tells us to lay aside in verse 25 includes silence, denial, and stuffing it—not just outright lying.

APPLY When have you given the devil an opportunity? What did he do?

_____

_____

_____

📖 Read Ephesians 4:29–32. What does the context of verse 30 imply about how we grieve the Holy Spirit? What behaviors show evidence that we are allowing the Holy Spirit to have His way in us? How do they affect community?

_____

_____

_____

The Holy Spirit is the giver of community. He is the glue binding us together. Love and community are His work. Jesus in John 17:23 prayed that our faith would be perfected in unity. The gift of the Holy Spirit is the Father's answer to the Son's prayer. The Spirit perfects our faith in the midst of community. We grieve the Holy Spirit when we speak words that do not edify, when we let bitterness, anger, and malice disrupt the unity He came to produce. Kindness, tenderness, and forgiveness are the Holy Spirit's fruit. The community interaction they generate causes the building up of the body in love.

APPLY How are kindness, tenderness, and forgiveness practiced in your community? By whom?

_____

_____

_____

Respond in prayer to what the Lord has shown you in this chapter.

_____

_____

_____

_____

_____

_____

_____

_____

_____

_____

Father, I adore You. I lay my life before You. I love You. I praise You for giving me all I need for life and godliness. I praise you for the gift of faith. I bless You for blessing me with every spiritual blessing in Christ. Thank You for choosing me, for adopting me, for redeeming and forgiving me. Thank You for sealing me in Him with the Holy Spirit.

I confess that I have not fully understood and embraced my union with Christ. My focus has been on myself and my own efforts to please and obey You. I have not seen Your hand in everything and have failed to take the opportunities You have provided for my spiritual development. I have too often chosen independence and individuality and failed to see the riches of the glory in the saints You have put in my life.

Father I pray with and for my community that you would strengthen us with power through Your Spirit so that Christ may dwell in our hearts through faith, and that we may know His love with all the saints. We pray that we will be filled up to all the fullness of God. We pray that You would dwell in us and work through us for the well-being of the whole creation.

Deliver us, we pray, from hopelessness. Deliver us from separation and alienation. Deliver us from anger, slothfulness, and gossip. Help us to recognize the enemy's attempts to cause disunity and accusations. Help us to learn Christ together and truly understand what it means to be members of one another. Bind us together in love for Your glory. Amen.

Works Cited

1. Susan Schaeffer Macaulay, *How to Be Your Own Selfish Pig* (London, Scripture Union, 1982), 82.

2. Edith Schaeffer, *L'Abri* (Wheaton, IL: Crossway Books, 1992), 16.

3. John Sanderson, *The Fruit of the Spirit* (Phillipsburg, NJ: P and R Publishing, 1985), 32.

4. Miroslav Volf, *Free of Charge* (Grand Rapids, MI: Zondervan, 2005), 44.

5. Ibid., 152.

6. Robert Webber, *Ancient-Future Evangelism* (Grand Rapids, MI: Baker Books, 2003), 75.

7. Ibid., 39.

3

Excellence

"At Redeemer Indy, we are trying to be more holistic in our understanding of what it means to pursue excellence. It is not being nice people who try to be good, rather it is fighting for God's justice, renewal, and excellence in all we do and say, in every sphere of our lives." Jason Dorsey, the pastor at Redeemer, explains the vision of their church to enter into Christ's work of bringing renewal to all things. Christ's cosmic redemptive work is making all things excellent, not only our spiritual lives, but our whole being, our work, our relationships, our communities, our cities, our world.

Five years ago this community purchased the historic First Presbyterian Church in downtown Indianapolis. The magnificent hundred-year-old building had been abandoned and was still in major disrepair. The previous owner had purchased the 60,000-square-foot facility, hoping to turn it into an art and cultural center. Although he poured two million dollars into the project, he had restored only three-quarters of the building before moving on. When the Redeemer congregation purchased the building, they did not abandon the artistic and cultural vision of the previous owner. Instead, they made an important decision that has shaped their church and helped to bring renewal to the city. The members continue to improve and renew the beautiful building for worship, but they also use it as a thriving artistic and cultural community for the common good of the entire city.

Redeemer Indy . . .

a community of excellence

Many members have also moved into the city center to renew old homes and to establish a community of hope for the healing and renewal of the city. Also, Pastor Dorsey and his wife Jenny send their four children to the local public school so they can work with others to bring renewal and excellence to the broken Indianapolis Public School system.

Like Redeemer Indy, we need a vision for excellence that by faith and hope sees the end product of Christ's cosmic renewal. But such renewal requires a life-long fight against decay and disrepair, or idolatry and lusts. The process is slow and will ultimately only be completed in the age to come. The process also requires community. We need the strength of a shared faith and the encouragement of others to continue to bring in the gift of God's excellence to a broken world.

Excellence

2 PETER 1:3–7

*"Seeing that His divine power has granted to us everything we need for life and godliness through the true knowledge of Him who called us to His own glory and **excellence** . . . that you might become partakers of the divine nature. . . . For this reason bringing in with diligence supply in the faith of y'all the **excellence** and in **excellence** the knowledge and in knowledge the self-control and in self-control the perseverance and in perseverance the godliness and in godliness the brotherly kindness and in brotherly kindness the love."*

(Author's Composite Translation)

THE DIVINE NATURE OF EXCELLENCE

The Greek New Testament uses the word *arete* only four times. *Arete* is translated *"excellencies"* in Peter's first letter (2:9) and again in 2 Peter 1:3 where it refers to God and is translated *"excellence."* The only other time *arete* is found in Greek manuscripts is in Philippians 4:8, where Paul tells us to think on things that are excellent. I believe the most compelling argument for translating *arete* as excellence is that it is a repeated use of the word in the same passage. When the same word is used twice in one paragraph, it is normally translated the same. The meaning of *arete* is watered down when it is translated as moral excellence, virtue, or goodness. I can see how translators may have felt compelled to lessen the impact of *arete* if they thought it was something we have to add to our faith. They may have thought, if we have to come up with it on our own, it better not be out of our reach, so let's just call it goodness. If, however, we see it as a gift from God, it can contain all the glory of the universe.

Our study of excellence will focus on Paul's letter to the community of Colosse. Even though the word *arete* is not found in the Greek manuscripts of the epistle, the letter's theme is Christ's surpassing excellence and how we must *put on* that excellency. Paul's metaphor of taking off and putting on is similar to Peter's metaphor of partaking of the divine nature. The Colossian community thought they needed to add traditions and rules to their faith. In contrast, Paul seeks to establish them in the sufficiency of Christ's excellence.

📖 Read Colossians 1:15-20. List all the descriptions of Christ in these verses.

_____

_____

_____

What do you think it means that He is the image of the invisible God?

_____

_____

_____

What does Genesis 1 tell us about the quality of what He created?

_____

_____

What does the fact that they were created by Him and for Him tell us?

_____

_____

_____

What do you think it means that all things hold together in Him?

_____

_____

_____

What is Christ's role in the church?

_____

_____

Paul's description of Christ helps us focus on His excellence.

 How does focusing on Christ's excellence help you appropriate more excellence in your own life?

_____

_____

_____

We know that God created us in His image, but that image was marred when we fell into sin. Salvation is all about restoring the image. Christ is the only way back to God, and through Him we become partakers of His divine nature. As we grow in a true knowledge of Him, He will impart His nature to us more and more.

📖 Read 2 Peter 1:3 and Colossians 1:12–14. What do you think it means that Christ has *"called us to his own glory and excellence"* (ESV)? How did He do that?

_____

_____

_____

_____

God has granted to us all we need for life and godliness through the true knowledge of His Son, who has called us *to* His own excellence. The New American Standard Bible says *"by"* His own excellence, but notice that the option in the notes says *"to."* The English Standard Version (ESV) translates it as *"to."* This is an intriguing distinction. Calling us *to* His excellence implies a destination or a change in nature. *By* His excellence would just imply cause.

Word Study
GOD'S EXCELLENCE

Vines Expository Dictionary defines *arete* as "whatever procures pre-eminent estimation for a person or thing." In other words, it is a quality of value, goodness, or beauty that achieves acclaim or praise. The word "moral" is not found in the Greek and is unnecessary if we interpret *arete* to refer to God's excellence.

Did You Know?
2 PETER 1:5

The translators of the Old Testament into Greek used *arete* only once. In Habakkuk 3:3 the Septuagint translates the Hebrew word *hod* as *arete*. English translators choose words like beauty, splendor, majesty, and so forth, to express the meaning of *hod*. I can't help but think Peter's choice to use this uncommon word, *arete*, in his list in 2 Peter 1:5 must have been intentional, and I wonder if choosing a common word like "goodness" misses that intent.

In Paul's letter to the Colossians, he explains that the Father has qualified us to share in an inheritance of light in His beloved Son's kingdom. Our redemption and forgiveness bring about an essential change not only in our standing but also in our natures. We become more like Christ as our knowledge of Him and intimacy with Him increases. This is the way He calls us to His excellence. It is a call to know Him more.

APPLY What do you think is the difference between excellence and perfectionism?

_____

_____

_____

If we don't understand that Peter's use of the word translated *"excellence"* in 2 Peter 1:5 refers to God's excellence, we could get pulled into perfectionism.

Author Donna Otto in her book *Between Women of God* contrasts the two:

Excellence is risk	Perfection is fear
Excellence is powerful	Perfection is anger and frustration
Excellence is spontaneous	Perfection is control
Excellence is accepting	Perfection is judgment
Excellence is giving	Perfection is taking
Excellence is confidence	Perfection is doubt
Excellence is flowing	Perfection is pressure
Excellence is journey	Perfection is destination[1]

Donna sees the difference. A journey to His excellence is a walk of faith. The pressure to add perfection (goodness, or moral virtue) to our faith will take us into negative repercussions.

📖 Read Colossians 1:19–23. What was Christ's goal in His incarnation and death according to these verses? How does that illustrate both His excellence and the excellence He wants to give us?

_____

_____

_____

_____

The goal of the Trinity was to reconcile all things to Himself. The incarnation brought the fullness of the Godhead into a man, and His death brought peace and the possibility of a renewed excellence back into the world.

There is a big difference between *"alienation, hostility, and evil"* and *"being holy, blameless, and beyond reproach."* We might imagine a change like that would take a lot of self-discipline and effort on our part. But according to the verses we are studying, Christ has done all the necessary work, and our part is to continue in the faith. This is why Peter says we supply excellence in our shared faith. Our effort is to continue in the faith and not move away from the hope of the gospel. As a community, we need to remind one another of that hope.

📖 Reread Colossians 1:13–14, 20 and 23. What is the hope of the gospel? How do you think we move away from it?

_____
_____
_____
_____

The gospel is stated in verse 20 of this passage: God has reconciled a fallen world to Himself through Christ, who made peace through the blood of His cross. The *hope* is that one day *all things* will be reconciled, redeemed, renewed, and delivered from the domain of darkness. We move away from hope when we see only the domain of darkness. We move away from hope when we let discouragement stop us from reclaiming what He has redeemed. We move away from hope when we let our guilt and shame define us. We move away from hope when we deny our sins and stop repenting. We move away from hope when we think God cannot forgive or restore us.

APPLY What are some ways you are prone to move away from the hope of the gospel?

_____
_____
_____

How can your community help you hold on to hope?

_____
_____
_____

WALKING IN FAITH: THE KEY TO EXCELLENCE

Before we read our first passage in Colossians for today, I want to point out that it serves as a prayer. The best measure of our faith is our prayer lives. The clearest indicator of how much we depend on God and not ourselves is the priority we give to prayer. We may claim to walk by faith, but if prayer isn't a major part of our lives, there is little reason to believe faith has much to do with the way we live.

📖 Read Colossians 1:9–14. How can we walk *"in a manner worthy of the Lord?"* Do you think that is a good description of excellence? What enables us to do this?

_____
_____
_____

"For it was the Father's good pleasure for all the fullness to dwell in Him, and through Him to reconcile all things to Himself."

Colossians 1:19–20

Excellence

DAY TWO

Our excellence is His gift to us, not the other way around.

Paul's first prayer request is for spiritual wisdom and understanding. He implies that we cannot "walk" until we know and understand. A cycle of knowing, understanding, walking, and bearing fruit, leads back to more knowing. Each time we cycle through, we increase our knowledge. Then in verses 11 through 14, Paul points out that all this is done in God's strength and power, not our own. We must thank Him for qualifying us. His work of delivering, transferring, redeeming, and forgiving enables us to walk in a manner worthy of the Lord. Our excellence is His gift to us, not the other way around.

APPLY Does your prayer life indicate dependency on God or too much independence?

_____

_____

How will it be different for you to give up trying to *"walk in a manner worthy of the Lord"* and to embrace Christ's qualifying work in you?

_____

_____

_____

How might the ceaseless prayers of others in your community help?

_____

_____

_____

Read Colossians 1:24–2:3. What mystery is Paul talking about in these verses? How does this help us understand what it means to partake of the divine nature?

_____

_____

_____

Paul uses the word *mystery* three times in this passage. In verse 26 he refers to the mystery that he preached. Then in verse 27 the mystery is described as *"Christ in you, the hope of glory."* Later in verse 2 of chapter 2, he speaks of *"a true knowledge of God's mystery, which is Christ."* Notice the progressive revelation of this mystery, first in the preaching of God's Word, then the sending His Spirit to be in us, and finally in Christ's giving us understanding, wisdom, and knowledge. In each case our part is to know and believe. When we believe, our hearts will be *"encouraged, having been knit together in love."* Partaking of the divine nature seems to happen by a combination of Paul's faithful stewardship of the gospel and God's mysterious working within the community of His people.

Read Colossians 2:6–7. How do we *"walk in Him"* according to these verses? What do you think it means to be established in the faith?

_____

_____

_____

_____

Here again we see that walking in Him means to be rooted and established in faith. Going back to our passage in 2 Peter 1, we remember that a shared faith supplies excellence. Walking in Him is living by faith and doing what He is doing with the community of faith. Remember, Christ, as the image of the invisible God, restores excellence to a fallen world in a cosmic redemptive work. As we walk in Him, He not only restores us to excellence (making us holy, blameless, and beyond reproach) but also involves us in His work of making *all things* a reflection of His excellence. As head over all things, He brings renewal to all things. He gave His life and was torn apart to bring all things back together. Walking in Him implies an active faith. It is going in the same direction as He is. This faith says, "If He worked and suffered in this way, I can work and suffer as a member of His body in a similar way, with the same goal."

 How are *you* going to walk in Him this week? How might your community help you to walk in Him?

_____

_____

_____

📖 Read Colossians 2:8–15. How do circumcision and burial prepare us for excellence? What connection can you see between forgiveness and excellence?

_____

_____

_____

In verse 8 Paul refers to pagan philosophies that can deceive believers. He may have had in mind the teachings of other world religions that suggest we can attain excellence by our own efforts, by living lives of "don'ts," or by paying for our debts through sacrifice and service. We have default modes in our fallen natures that make us think that we must work for our redemption. Paul convincingly argues that we have been made complete in Christ. In Him the fullness of Deity dwells, in other words, the excellence we long for is found in Him. When we by faith are united to Him, He cuts away the body of flesh. He removes all the burdens of our transgressions and debts. The "accuser of the brethren" can no longer claim that we belong to his domain of darkness. Our baptism pictures how we are transferred into His kingdom, totally forgiven and cleansed of sin. Living in pursuit of excellence is now possible by His grace.

 How much do pagan philosophies deceive you and impact the way you think about obtaining excellence or perfection?

_____

_____

_____

"As you therefore have received Christ Jesus the Lord, so walk in Him, having been firmly rooted and now being built up in Him and established in your faith."

Colossians 2:5–6

EXCELLENCE, NOT RULE KEEPING

Yesterday we learned we are made complete in Christ. We are to walk in Him and enjoy the riches of the mystery that He is in us. This is how we partake of His excellence. Today we will read on in Paul's letter and focus on the contrast between religion and a "partaking" relationship. Most religions and even many Christian churches teach specific steps we must take to become holy or to obtain some level of virtue. As you read, study, and discuss the verses for today, focus on the difference between religion and the relationships to which Paul calls us.

Read Colossians 2:11–13. In the process Paul describes in these verses, who is active, and who is passive? How have you experienced Christ's circumcision of your flesh? What does it mean to you that *"He made you alive together with Him"*?

_____

_____

_____

_____

Christ's work of removing our sinful natures is a continuing process. He has always been very gentle with me, first convicting me of a certain sin, then bringing me to repentance and confession. His assurance of forgiveness gives me the courage to let go of sinful habits, and His grace enables me to form new godly habits. His love permeates the whole process and quickens new life in me.

Read Colossians 2:14–17, 23. How are we to respond to those who tell us that we can obtain excellence by keeping certain rules and regulations? What do you think Paul means by *shadow and substance*?

_____

_____

_____

_____

Although legalists may judge us, we do not have to listen to them. Others may try to convince us that we can obtain excellence by self-abasement, or supernatural experiences, or false worship. Paul calls all these efforts mere shadows. No self-made religions can change our self-centered fleshly indulgences into a pursuit of divine excellence.

Hebrews 10:1 helps us understand Paul's reference to the word "shadow." There we learn that the law was *"only a shadow of the good things to come and not the very form of things."* God gave the Israelites rules and regulations to show them their sin and need of a redeemer. The lamb an Israelite brought to the altar was a shadow of the sacrifice Jesus would one day make. Keeping the law or following a list of rules is not the way to excellence. We are defrauded of the real prize of excellence when we let someone convince us of any substance apart from Christ.

"Law guides change, but cannot produce it."

—Michael Kelly, my pastor

Substance refers to reality. When Paul says *"the substance belongs to Christ"* he means that Christ is the real thing. He alone is the image of the invisible God; only in Him does the fullness of Deity dwell. And only in our union with Him can we partake of the divine nature of excellence.

APPLY Would you describe the church in which you grew up or the training you received as a child as legalistic? What were some particular aspects of that training?

_____

_____

_____

Why do you think we are so prone to rule keeping?

_____

_____

_____

We find it easier to check off a list of dos and don'ts than to truly trust God. We can maintain a measure of control by following a list, but we must fully surrender when we walk with Christ.

Read Colossians 2:18–19. Why is *"holding fast to the head"* so important? What do you think that means?

_____

_____

_____

_____

Again, we can better understand this peculiar phrase by looking at another passage of Scripture. In Ephesians 1:22–23 Paul teaches us that God put all things under Christ's feet and *"gave Him as head over all things to the church, which is His body."* Also, remember Colossians 1:18 explains that Christ is the *"head of the body, the church."* Holding fast to Christ as our head means to take our rightful position under him. As part of His body, we should submit to Him in everything. Only when we realize that we have no substance apart from Him, no hope without Him, and no way to God but through Him can we let go of all else and hold fast to Him. Only then can we become more aware of His claim and purposes in our lives.

APPLY In what ways can we as a community diligently hold fast to Christ, the Head? How can we encourage each other to hold fast?

_____

_____

_____

_____

"And He put all things in subjection under His feet, and gave Him as head over all things to the church, which is His body, the fullness of Him who fills all in all."

Ephesians 1:22–23

PUTTING OFF AND ON

In the early 1800s, Thomas Chalmers preached a famous sermon entitled "The Expulsive Power of a New Affection." In it he explained how we put off the old self and put on the new.

> The heart is not so constituted with an innate elasticity of its own to cast the world away from it. The only way to dispossess it of an old affection is by the expulsive power of a new one. . . . We know of no other way by which to keep the love of the world out of our heart, than to keep in our hearts the love of God—and no other way by which to keep our hearts in the love of God, than building ourselves up on our most holy faith. . . . To try this without faith is to work without the right tool.[2]

Chalmers' words underline the importance of faith. Our pursuit of excellence must take place in the arena of faith. Remember, we supply excellence in our shared faith. As we encourage one another with the truth that God loves each of us, and grow in our love for one another, our hearts are more and more filled with His love, and the love of the world is effectively put off.

📖 Read Colossians 3:1–5. What do *"dying with Christ"* and *"being raised up with Christ"* have to do with partaking of His excellence? What do you think Paul means by these statements?

_____

_____

_____

_____

We partake of the divine nature of excellence by faith. First we believe Christ died for our sins. But these verses tell us we must also believe that we died with Him, and therefore can be dead to our sins. Furthermore, we are to believe that we are already raised with Christ. Then by faith we see what Christ has done for us and is doing in us. When by faith we grab hold of these truths, they enable us to live as if they are true.

APPLY In what ways could we help one another identify our true affections?

_____

_____

_____

What things do you need help in truly believing?

_____

_____

_____

📖 Read Colossians 3:5–8. How do we put to death our idolatries?

_____

_____

_____

In our old nature, we tried to find love wherever we could and to fill our emptiness with anything that promised satisfaction. We sought to fulfill every desire and passion that motivated us and wanted everything we saw others enjoying. Life in pursuit of this kind of happiness is idolatry. We make passions and fleshly desires our idols.

To *"consider the members of your earthly body as dead"* to sin is a way to kill idolatry. Whenever you are tempted to fulfill an evil desire, you must *consider*. Take a trip in your mind with the part of your body that wants something. Go to the cross and see three things: 1) Christ dying for that sin; 2) your old self dying with Christ; 3) your nailing that desire to the cross. Only the power of the cross can give you victory over sin.

Notice that sheer willpower or determination does not keep us from sin. Rather, if we set our minds on Christ, and consider His death on the cross, then by faith we can put off the old life and put on the new life of Christ. We often prefer determination even though it doesn't work because it does not take faith. When determination fails we go to denial. We either deny it is sin or we deny we have a problem with it. And always we deny the power of the cross. *"By grace, through faith"* is our only hope. The grace of God working in us enables us to obey. Our faith receives that grace and works it out in our day-to-day living and in our struggles with sin.

APPLY What specific idols do you need to put to death in your life? How can the shared faith of your community help you put them to death?

_____

_____

_____

When is it most difficult for you to control your tongue? How can we help one another put away the sins of the tongue?

_____

_____

_____

📖 Read Colossians 3:9–11. Why does Paul tell us not to lie to one another? What do you think is the most common way we do this? How do distinctions encourage it?

_____

_____

_____

_____

I think the most common way I lie to others is by the pretense I try to maintain, especially around other Christians I want to impress. It is part of my human nature to want to look better than I am, and to compare myself with others more favorably. Paul's point here is that there are no distinctions when Christ is all and in us all. We are all on a completely level playing field, so we don't have to pretend we are better than others. We can all admit that apart from Christ we are miserable sinners. Best-selling author Lauren Winner points out:

Doctrine
HIDDEN WITH CHRIST IN GOD

When we partake of Christ's divine nature, He becomes our new life. His desires become our desires, and we live to serve Him. If our lives are hidden with Christ in God, we are free from the dominion of darkness and are no longer slaves to our sin and evil passions. By the strength of His power in us we can say no to sin.

Extra Mile
THE BATTLE OF THE TONGUE

James in his letter to the early church called the tongue a fire, set on fire by hell, and said no human being can tame it. But in verse 8 Paul simply tells us to put away *anger, wrath, malice, slander, and abusive speech.* We can do this only by faith. The battle takes place primarily in our minds. In verse 1 of this chapter, Paul tells us to keep seeking the things above, and in verse 2 he says, *"Set your mind on the things above."* This is similar to James's advice in chapter 3 of his letter. There James contrasts the wisdom from above with natural or demonic wisdom. The implication is that we can choose which wisdom to listen to, and set our minds on. We learn to control our tongues by faith as we put away or refuse to listen to anger and wrath and choose rather to set our minds on the *"pure, peaceable, gentle, and reasonable"* wisdom from above.

The Bible tells us to talk to one another about what is really going on in our lives . . . because what's going on in my life is already your concern, by dint of the baptism that made me your sister, my joys are your joys and my crises are your crises. We are called to speak to one another lovingly, to be sure, and with edifying, rather than gossipy or hurtful, goals. But we are called nonetheless to transform seemingly private matters into communal matters . . . speaking to one another is just one (admittedly risky) instance of a larger piece of Christian discipleship: being in community with each other.[3]

 APPLY What is the most common way you lie to others?

_____

_____

📖 Read Colossians 3:12–17. What do we "*put on*"? How do you think we do it?

_____

_____

_____

This long list of characteristics is a description of the new self Paul refers to in verse 10, where he says we are *"being renewed to a true knowledge according to the image of the One who created us."* That is simply another way of saying we partake of His divine nature as we put on our new selves. Compassion, kindness, humility, gentleness, patience and forgiveness are all part of God's excellence. Love, unity, and peace are the results of living by faith and partaking of His divine nature. We give thanks, because it is all His work and gifts to us. We let His Word richly dwell within us, because it is the power that works within us. We admonish one another in community, because that is part of how we put on the new self. When we do everything in the name of the Lord Jesus, we partake of His excellence.

 APPLY How often do you find yourself praising and thanking God?

_____

_____

Excellence

DAY FIVE

EXCELLENT RELATIONSHIPS

Jonathan Edwards, one of the most well known pastors in the eighteenth century, was also a prolific writer. He helps us think of more possibilities about the meaning of the word excellence when he wrote the following words:

Excellency is the consent of being to being—the essence of love and beauty . . . The consent of bodies to one another and the harmony that is among them is but the shadow of excellency. The highest excellency, therefore, must be the consent of spirits to one another.[4]

Edwards' thoughts on excellency help us understand how community plays an integral part in our partaking of excellence. In the last part of the letter to the Colossians, Paul zeroes in on their relationships with one another. He gives practical and cutting-edge advice to help them improve all their relationships. His words also apply to us. Inspired by the Holy Spirit, they are still living and active. We do well to study them carefully and encourage one another to pray and partake of Christ's excellence in every relationship.

📖 Read Colossians 3:18–21. What does excellence in the home look like?

_____

_____

Paul's words in these verses bring to my mind what Edwards wrote about excellence. These verses describe harmony in the home, or what he called "the consent of spirits to one another." God has ordained certain structure and roles in the family to help us maintain harmony. When we submit to His design we find the joy of excellence.

(APPLY) Describe and evaluate the relationships in your home. Can you say they are excellent?

_____

_____

_____

📖 Read Colossians 3:22—4:1. What does excellence in the workplace look like?

_____

_____

_____

The movie *Remains of the Day* illustrates the difference between doing ones work *"heartily"* and doing it merely to please others. In this film, the butler, Mr. Stinson, is a perfectionist, and he cannot comprehend a true excellence that results in harmony, love, and beauty. The housekeeper tries to reach out to him and show him a little heart, but he is totally blind to it. Work that is done with the heart manifests the love of God and others in the work itself. The relationships among the workers and their masters also honor God.

(APPLY) Do you know anyone who does their work *"heartily, as for the Lord"*? What makes them different from other workers?

_____

_____

_____

📖 Read Colossians 4:2–4, 12. How can we promote excellence in the church?

_____

_____

_____

"Whatever you do, do your work heartily, as for the Lord rather than for men."

Colossians 3:23

As we pointed out in the beginning of Day Two, walking in faith is the key to excellence, and the best measure of our faith is our prayer lives. Paul again calls the church of Colosse to prayer, this time specifically to pray for him. If we long for excellence in our churches, it is critical that we be devoted to prayer, especially for our leaders. Those who *"speak forth the mystery of Christ"* always need our prayers.

APPLY How much of your time together is devoted to prayer for your church and its leaders?

_____

_____

Read Colossians 4:5–6. What does excellence in the midst of the world look like?

_____

_____

Think of these words not only as they apply to you personally, but also to the church community. How can we conduct ourselves corporately in a way that makes the most of our opportunities to impact those around us? Because she understands the role the church plays and can so eloquently describe it, I again quote Lauren Winner:

> As the church, we tell the story of creation and redemption. . . . We animate the story through confession and confrontation. We embroider the story with practical tips that help people manage and express desire. We live the story through a series of institutions that display redemption to the world and enable the gospel to transform God's people through sacrament, and hospitality, and prayer. The church serves as a narrator reminding ourselves who we are, and why we do what we do. [5]

APPLY In what ways is your church acting as salt and light in the larger community? Are you making the most of every opportunity?

_____

_____

_____

Let us complete this chapter by praying earnestly that God would restore excellence in His kingdom and to the world. Please write your prayer in the space provided.

_____

_____

_____

_____

_____

_____

_____

If we long for excellence in our churches, it is critical that we be devoted to prayer for our leaders.

Father, we praise You for Your excellence. All glory, laud, and honor are Yours. We celebrate Your amazing plan to redeem a people who will be enabled by Your grace to work with You in restoring excellence to a fallen world.

We confess that our faith is too small, that we are still blinded to so much of what You offer us. Please forgive our self-centeredness and ever-returning desire to produce our own excellence. We think our perfectionism somehow honors You, when in fact it spurns Your grace and ignores Your provisions. Please forgive us when we move away from the hope of the gospel. Help us encourage one another to hold on to hope. Lord, please fill us with the knowledge of Your will in all spiritual wisdom and understanding. Lead us to walk in a manner worthy of You. May all we do please You and bear fruit in Your name. Strengthen us with all power according to Your glorious might. May we be steadfast, patient, and joyously thankful.

Deliver us, O Lord, from the temptation to try to keep Your law without holding fast to Christ. Deliver us from lukewarmness. Rescue us from this fallen world of sin and darkness. Bring us into Your kingdom of light and enable us to put to death all our idolatries. Heal our relationships and restore excellence among us, we pray. In Jesus' name and for His glory.

Works Cited

1. Donna Otto, *Between Women of God* (Eugene, OR: Harvest House, 1995), 41.

2. Thomas Chalmers, *Chalmers' Sermons*, vol. 2 (New York: Robert Carter, 1846), 274, 277.

3. Lauren Winner, *Real Sex* (Grand Rapids, MI: Baker Publishing Group, 2005), 53.

4. George Marsden, *Jonathan Edwards: A Life* (New Haven, CT: Yale University Press, 2003), 78.

5. Winner, 59.

Notes

4

Knowledge

The World Team Missions organization has founded a community for Latin American church planting that weds discipleship and community in a dynamic way. They chose their name from the Spanish word for "house" and the Hebrew word for "knowledge of God." These missionaries formed **Casa Yada** because old models of equipping and training leaders in foreign countries were failing. Seeking to develop a model that would not only inform minds but also transform hearts, they focus on the development of deep spiritual character. Their vision is to provide hands-on training for national leaders within the context of community.

Actually, living in intentional community is the principal component of this mission's view of discipleship. Seasoned missionaries live in homes together with families of national church leaders. Choosing a community-based model as opposed to a campus-based seminary model replaces the emphasis on knowledge with a relationally centered, discipling approach. The central focus is on forming spiritual character, vision, and integrity. Intellectual knowledge and the development of leadership skills are further down on their priority list. Seeking to create an environment that encourages encounters with Christ, they explain. "There is no formula that is the answer. There is no technique that leads us to a solution. There is only a Person who offers us life through intimacy with Himself."[1] These missionaries have found that living and walking with those they seek to train is the best way to create

Casa Yada . . .

. . . a community of knowledge

this environment. Casa Yada calls this living "incarnationally" as they "live out the reality of the gospel in transparent relationships with trainees and their families." The plan is to hand over the leadership of the project in eight years to Latin American nationals discipled within the community model. Nationals will be most effective in their own countries in building similar communities.

CHRIST'S KNOWLEDGE

The incarnation of Christ, the fact that God became man and lived among us, was God's clearest revelation of Himself to us. We can know God because of Christ's incarnation. He humbled Himself and became a man, entering into our pain, our temptations, our sorrows, in order to invite us into His world of love and fellowship. In John 20:21, Jesus tells His disciples, *"As the Father has sent Me, even so send I you"* (KJV). What if He meant He was sending us to live incarnationally, as Casa Yada calls it? How would that change our approach to ministry? I think it's the difference between sending money to AIDS orphans in Africa and going to hold, rock, and love those sorrowful children. At least it is leaving the virtual reality of television relationships to spend time with real neighbors. As you consider the life of Christ, keep your mind and heart open to the possibility of your living more incarnationally.

📖 Read Hebrews 1:1–3 and John 1:18; 6:46. In what way was Jesus' knowledge of God different than the prophets?

_____

_____

_____

2 PETER 1:3–7

*"Seeing that His divine power has granted to us everything we need for life and godliness through the true **knowledge** of Him who called us . . . that you might become partakers of the divine nature. . . . For this reason bringing in with diligence supply in the faith of y'all the excellence and in excellence the **knowledge** and in **knowledge** the self-control and in self-control the perseverance and in perseverance the godliness and in godliness the brotherly kindness and in brotherly kindness the love."*

(Author's Composite Translation)

Jesus knew His Father intimately. The exact imprint of His Father's nature was on Him. God revealed His will by speaking to the prophets, but He revealed His whole nature by sending and speaking through His Son. The prophets gave the Word, but Jesus was the Word.

📖 Read Hebrews 2:14–18 and 2 Peter 1:4. How did taking the form of humanity help Jesus to know us better? Verse 14 tells us He partook of our nature, how does that relate to our partaking of His nature? How does living incarnationally help us know Him and one another better?

_____

_____

_____

_____

Do you remember the old Indian saying that you cannot know a person until you have walked a mile in his moccasins? In His incarnation Jesus came down to do more than walk a mile with us. He walked all the way to the cross for us. He was made like us in all things to become a merciful and faithful high priest for us. Now that He has made propitiation for our sins, He calls us to walk with Him and be more and more made like Him. He is sending us into the world of our neighbors, to be priests to them and help them to know God.

APPLY Can you think of people you know who are living incarnationally? How do they do it?

_____

_____

_____

What would it take for you to love others so much that you would be willing to enter into their lives and their struggles?

_____

_____

_____

It seems to me that I need a stronger connection to Christ in order to live incarnationally. Because I get to know Christ better through prayer, His Word, His Spirit, and His people I want to make them priorities in my life. I also need to be willing to comfort others in their suffering and be with them in their grief.

Read John 5:19; 7:16, 28-29; 8:28–29 and Hebrews 3:1–2. How did Jesus' knowledge of the Father impact His life? What did faithfulness look like for Him? How does our consideration of Him help us partake of our heavenly calling?

_____

_____

_____

_____

Jesus could see what His Father was doing. He could hear what the Father was saying. Even though He was living here on earth, He was abiding with the Father. Our calling is to fix our eyes on Jesus (Hebrews 12:2). In considering Him, we are to see what He is doing, to hear what He says to us, and to fix our eyes on Him even as He fixed His eyes on the Father. We are called to know Him intimately, and to be faithful to the One who has called us, just as He was faithful to the One who appointed Him.

APPLY How does your faithfulness compare to Christ's? In what ways could we partake of His faithfulness?

_____

_____

_____

Read John 10:14–15, 30, 38 and 17:11, 20–21. What kind of relationship did Jesus have with His Father? How can that be mirrored in our relationship with Jesus and with one another?

_____

_____

_____

Word Study
NATURE

The Greek word _phusis_ signifies the natural powers or constitution of a person. We know from our study of 2 Peter 1 that God's nature includes excellence, knowledge, self-control, perseverance, godliness, brotherly kindness, and love. On the other hand, human nature, because of sin, includes frailty, ignorance, temptation, failure, ungodliness, selfishness, and indifference towards others. As we partake of the divine nature in community we become more like Him and are less controlled by our own base natures.

Jesus knows us, and we are to know Him, even as the Father knows Him and He knows the Father. He claimed to be one with the Father and said the Father was in Him and He was in the Father. Then He prayed that we might all be one, even as the Trinity is one. Verse 20 makes it clear that He was praying for you and me as well as for the twelve disciples. If we could truly grasp the amazing scope of this prayer and its far-reaching ramifications, it would explode in an astonishing display of love, connection, and intimacy.

 Why do you think Jesus was so concerned that we be one?

_____

_____

_____

Colossians 2:2–3 implies we can only attain true knowledge of Christ if our hearts have been knit together in love. Why do you think that is necessary?

_____

_____

_____

 Word Study
KNOWLEDGE

The American Heritage Dictionary tells us that knowledge is "familiarity, awareness, or understanding gained through experience or study." Proverbs 9:10 says, *"The fear of the LORD is the beginning of wisdom, and the knowledge of the Holy One is understanding."* The context of our passage in 2 Peter indicates the author has in mind the knowledge of God in Christ. Knowledge could refer to many things, but by his repeated use of the word in verses 2, 3, and 8 of chapter 1, Peter implies that we are to supply the knowledge of the Holy One in our shared faith. Verse 2 tells us that we receive grace and peace through that knowledge. In verse 3 Peter refers to the true knowledge of Him who has called us, and tells us that we receive everything we need for life and godliness through that knowledge. Then again in verse 8 Peter ties our fruitfulness to our knowledge of Christ.

KNOWING CHRIST

In Day One we discussed how Christ's intimate knowledge both of the Father and of humanity was revealed in His incarnation. Today we will move on with the writer to the Hebrews to explore how our knowledge of Jesus Christ and His covenant enables us to partake of His divine nature and bear fruit for His glory. In Hebrews 3 and 4 the writer contrasts the failure of the Israelites and the hope we have for success. Look carefully to find the differences.

📖 Read Hebrews 3:5–14. In what ways did the Israelites fail? How does the fact that Christ is a Son over us (verse 6) and we are partakers of Him (verse 14) give us hope for success? What do you think it means to be *"partakers of Christ?"*

_____

_____

_____

Even though the Israelites were a community, it was not always a community of faith. Sometimes they encouraged one another to disobey rather than to trust God. They hardened their hearts when He spoke to them. Since they did not know God's ways, they went astray in their hearts. In contrast, we are given the challenge in this passage to encourage one another daily, to partake of Christ together, and make sure that none of those in our community fail to hear His voice, know His ways, and enter His rest.

 Which is more difficult for you: hearing His voice, knowing His ways, or entering His rest?

_____

_____

_____

How could your community help you more with what you find difficult?

_____

_____

📖 Read Hebrews 4:1, 10–11. What do you think it means to enter His rest?

_____

_____

_____

I believe His rest has both a present and a future application. We can diligently hold onto Christ now so that one day we will enter into our promised land of the new heavens and the new earth—but I believe we can also enter a rest today. Author Andrew Murray explains it this way,

> It is the rest in which you can live every hour, free from care and anxiety, free from weariness and wanderings, always resting in the rest that trusts God for all. Believe this. Then cease from you own works, and bow in deep humility and helplessness of all good, as nothing before God.[2]

APPLY What are some ways we could encourage each other to enter this rest, as well as our final rest.

_____

_____

_____

📖 Read Hebrews 4:12–13. What do these verses have to do with increasing our knowledge of Christ and entering His rest?

_____

_____

_____

These verses tell us to submit to the scalpel of His Word. This is so important in our pursuit of knowing Christ and His ways. The Israelites refused to hear His word, and sometimes we also close our hearts to what He says to us. We need the accountability to our community of faith to keep us in the Word, open and laid bare before its piercing truth, and willing to be judged by its convicting application.

📖 Read Hebrews 4:14–16. How does the fact that Jesus is our great High Priest help us *hold fast our confession?*

_____

_____

_____

Put Yourself in Their Shoes
OUR ADVANTAGES

We sometimes think of the people of ancient Israel as being such losers, but imagine how difficult it was for them. Which of the following gifts do you have and depend on that they did not have?

❑ Jesus Christ

❑ The Holy Spirit

❑ The printed Word of God

❑ A community of faith

"For the word of God is living and active and sharper than any two-edged sword ... and there is no creature hidden from His sight but all things are open and laid bare to the eyes of Him with whom we have to do."

Hebrews 4:12–13

I love that this pronoun is plural. I am not sure I could hold to a confession that was mine alone. Not only does my High Priest enable me to overcome my weaknesses and lack of faith, but my brothers and sisters confess their faith with me each week as a part of our corporate worship. As we draw near to the throne of grace together, we find grace. In the Old Testament the priests drew near to the mercy seat to find mercy. We have it even better. We not only receive the mercy and forgiveness of God, but we can draw near to the throne of grace and also find grace to enable us to live and walk in the power of the Holy Spirit. And we have the privilege of doing it together.

 Our times of prayer together in our small groups can and should be the most powerful and enabling times of our lives. Are they? What might need to change?

_____

_____

_____

Knowledge

DAY THREE

KNOWING OUR CALLING

One of the most important things we need to know for sure is that Christ has personally called us. The word *calling* or *called* is used twice in our original passage in 2 Peter 1. Verse 3 tells us the Lord has granted to us all we need for life and godliness through the true knowledge of Him who *called* us. Then again in verse 10 he tells us we must be diligent to make certain about His *calling* and choosing us. Paul makes a similar statement in his prayer in Ephesians 1:17–18, when he asks the Father to give the Ephesians a spirit of wisdom and of revelation in the knowledge of Him, that the eyes of their heart would be enlightened so that they might know the hope of His *calling*. The writer to the community of the Hebrews devotes a whole chapter to help them grapple with the big question of their eternal security in the hope of their calling.

📖 Read Hebrews 6:1–8. How would you describe the basic question being addressed in these verses? Why would that be important for pressing on to maturity?

_____

_____

_____

In contrast to Christians in the centuries preceding ours, many of us today are far less concerned about pressing on to spiritual maturity. We have been sold a bill of goods that assures us we are secure in our salvation because we have simply chosen Christ. This human-centered approach to understanding the way of salvation has led to a false assurance for many. When Scripture tells us we must make sure we know that Christ has called and chosen us, it underlines the fact that He initiates our salvation rather than our choosing Him. And it is vitally important that we know for sure that He has called us.

In the second century, Ignatius, the bishop of Antioch, wrote letters to churches that were concerned about finding the way to become "real disciples" and "genuine Christians." He wrote,

> Have a thorough belief in Jesus Christ and love him. That is the beginning and end of life: faith the beginning and love the end. And when the two are united you have God, and everything else that has to do with real goodness is dependent on them . . . "The tree is known by its fruit." Similarly, those who profess to be Christ's will be recognized by their actions. For what matters is not a momentary act of professing, but being persistently motivated by faith.[3]

A common misconception of our day is the teaching that our salvation is based on decisions we make. It teaches that if we "accept Jesus" or "say the sinner's prayer" we are eternally secure. Our assurance of salvation can never be based on something we have done. If the Father has planted us, the Son has summoned us, and the Spirit has borne fruit in us, then we can know we are saved. We know the Father as our Father. We know the Son as our Savior and Lord. We know the Spirit working in and through us.

 How are you going to make your calling and election sure?

_____

_____

📖 Read Hebrews 6:9–12. What things accompany salvation? What implications can be made about community?

_____

_____

_____

The earlier quote from Ignatius reminded us of Christ's statement in Matthew 12:33 that we can know a tree by its fruit. This can be applied not only to discerning the saving faith of other believers but can also help us know for sure about our own calling and salvation. First John 3 teaches we can know we are children of God by our love; and we can know He abides in us by the fruit He bears in us. In this passage in Hebrews it is the love and ministry of the Christians that convinces the writer that they are not going to fall away. But verse 11 mentions that our continued diligence to the end is necessary for full assurance.

 How does seeing the things that accompany salvation in our lives give us assurance of our calling? What things do you see in your life?

_____

_____

_____

📖 Read Hebrews 6:13–20. What is the author's argument in this passage? What is the hope we lay hold of? What promise of God is being referred to? How does this apply to us?

_____

_____

If the Father has planted us, the Son has summoned us, and the Spirit has borne fruit in us, then we can know we are saved. We know the Father as our Father. We know the Son as our Savior and Lord. We know the Spirit working in and through us.

THE DAY OF ATONEMENT

We are assured every time we confess our sins that they are forgiven (1 John 1:9), but the Israelites had that assurance only once a year, on the Day of Atonement. On that day, the high priest took the sacrifice for their sins into the Holy of Holies, the very presence of God, while the people waited anxiously to see if God would accept the sacrifice and forgive their sins. They would sometimes tie a rope around the priest's foot, so they could drag him out if the Lord did not accept the sacrifice and struck him dead. His reappearance (like a resurrection) relieved their fears and gave them hope for another year.

Knowledge

DAY FOUR

_____

_____

We can know God because He has revealed Himself in His covenant promises. God's purpose is unchangeable—He promised to bless and multiply Abraham, and He promises to bless us. He made a people of God out of Abraham's heirs, and He is making a people of God out of Christ's heirs. We can "know that we know" or have a calm inner assurance because of the strong encouragement, the anchor of hope, the sure foundation we have in Christ. As our High Priest, He has entered as a forerunner into the very presence of God for us. Just as the Israelites hope went with their priest when he went into the Holy of Holies, and they waited expectantly for his return and proclamation that atonement had been made for their sins, our hope is in Christ. By His resurrection, He proclaimed that the atonement had been made and the Father was satisfied. Our relationship with Him, our knowledge of Him, and our union with Him assures us that God the Father welcomes us into His presence.

APPLY What is the hope of your calling? Why do you need to pray that God will *"open the eyes of your heart"* to see it (Ephesians 1:18)?

_____

_____

_____

How can others in your community help you to see it?

_____

_____

Do you know many people who may have a false security in their own decision to choose Christ? In what ways might you help them to see the importance of making their calling and election sure?

_____

_____

_____

KNOWLEDGE IN COMMUNITY

So far in this chapter, we have looked at how we can know God, know Christ, and know our calling. In each lesson we have seen how community can enhance and enrich our knowledge. As the following quote from Cyprian, one of the early church fathers, points out, we all need the church community to help us grow in our knowledge of God: "You cannot have God for your father if you have not the church for your mother."[4]

Author Robert Webber makes the same point in a graphic way—he calls the church a womb for disciple making. He explains that the church's witness is not in words alone. It not only speaks God's message, but it also embodies the very reality of God. He gives the following examples to prove his point:

- The church's experience of community reflects the eternal relationship of Father, Son, and Spirit.

- The church's central focus on Jesus affirms it as a continuous witness to the presence of Jesus.

- The experience within the church of love, redemption, reconciliation, and peace is all a reflection of the redeeming work of Jesus.

- The way of following Jesus, dealing with evil, and caring for the poor and needy are all signs of discipleship.[5]

Keep this picture in mind as you read the verses from Hebrews listed below. Think not only about how much you need the church, but also how you and your community can do a better job of making disciples: helping others know the reality of God and His Son, Jesus Christ, and all that He taught us.

📖 Read Hebrews 11:8–10, 13–16; 1 Peter 2:4–5 and Revelation 21:1–3. What is God building, and how are our faith choices similar to Abraham's? In what ways might we look for the city God is building?

_____

_____

_____

_____

Put Yourself in Their Shoes
THE CITY GOD IS BUILDING

Kevin VandenBrink, my former pastor, once said he liked to worship in a racially diverse community because it more clearly reflects the worship in heaven. He figured if God was building a racially diverse city in heaven he needed to practice worshiping with many different people groups. He now pastors a church in St. Louis filled with refugees from many different nations.

Probably the most famous quote from the popular *Experiencing God* Bible study (Nashville, TN: LifeWay, 1990) is, "We need to join God in doing what He is doing." That idea should bring to mind all kinds of ways we can look for the city God is building and join Him there. Your discussion of this question will likely come up with many different applications.

For example, whenever our family grappled with a decision of moving to a new place, our first consideration was not only what job opportunities we would find there, but also what good churches were in the area. We would never make a move and then look for a church. I believe that was one way we were looking for God's city.

APPLY In what ways do you look for the city God is building?

_____

_____

_____

📖 Read Hebrews 11:24–26. How was Moses' choice similar to the ones we need to make between time with community or with the pleasures of this life?

_____

_____

_____

_____

"By faith Moses, when he had grown up, refused to be called the son of Pharaoh's daughter; choosing rather to endure ill-treatment with the people of God, than to enjoy the passing pleasures of sin."

Hebrews 11:24–25

Moses' choice to be with God's people, even if that proved to be painful, is an example we should remember when we face **any** decision, not just major life-changing ones. For example, when I was driving to my community group meeting one night, I thought, *I really don't feel like going tonight. I would much rather curl up by myself with a good book*. Because I am an introvert, groups don't attract me. But because I am a Christian, I know I need to be with God's people. Then I remembered all the others in my group. I knew many of them probably would like to enjoy other pleasures too but chose to come and be with the rest of us. Being together would help us know Christ more, and would continue building the love He intended for us to enjoy. Besides, they were studying this chapter and I needed to be there.

That reminds me of the story of the mother who tried to wake up her son for church one Sunday morning. He complained that he didn't want to go, and just didn't feel like it that morning. "Besides," he pointed out, "no one likes me there anymore." "But you have to go," his mother chided. "Why," he asked. "Because you are the pastor, and must preach this morning."

APPLY What are some of the decisions you have made recently that reflect your commitment to Christ and to community?

_____

_____

_____

Conversely, what decisions have you made that indicate you have some way to go, and God isn't through with you yet?

_____

_____

_____

📖 Read Hebrews 12:12–17. What is the community's responsibility according to these verses?

_____

_____

_____

These verses are not just written to individuals calling them to personal pursuits of peace and holiness. We are to pursue peace and holiness in our relationships with one another. The hands, knees, limbs, and joints refer to parts of the body of Christ, or brothers and sisters in our community, who suffer and need our care and ministry. Furthermore, it is not just the responsibility of leadership to see that *"no one comes short of the grace of God."* Although leaders may feel the burden more acutely, these words are written to us all.

Eugene Peterson's commentary on Psalm 133 gives a great description of the kind of community we should long for. Read the verses in the sidebar and meditate on the following:

> Oil throughout Scripture, is a sign of God's presence, a symbol of the Spirit of God. . . . There is a quality of warmth and ease in God's community which contrasts with the icy coldness and hard surfaces of people who jostle each other in mobs and crowds. But more particularly

"Behold, how good and how pleasant it is for brothers to dwell together in unity? It is like the precious oil upon the head, coming down upon the beard, even Aaron's beard, coming down upon the edge of his robes."

Psalms 133:1–2

here the oil is an anointing oil, marking the person as a priest. Living together means seeing the oil flow over the head, down the face, through the beard, onto the shoulders of the other—and when I see that I know that my brother, my sister, is my priest. When we see the other as God's anointed, our relationships are profoundly affected. . . . Christ anoints us with his Spirit. We are set apart for service to one another. We mediate to one another the mysteries of God. We represent to one another the address of God. We are priests who speak God's Word and share Christ's sacrifice.[6]

APPLY What are some ways you can strengthen weak hands or feeble knees in your community?

_____

_____

_____

How do you make straight paths for others in the church?

_____

_____

_____

What does it mean to you that you are a priest for the others in your community?

_____

_____

_____

KNOWING THE FATHER'S LOVE

I received an e-mail recently from a missionary friend, Donovan Graham, posing an intriguing question. He had read a book by Nancy Verrier called *The Primal Wound: Understanding the Adopted Child.* In this book Verrier explains how adopted children often find it hard to fully accept and be satisfied in the love of the adoptive parents, even when they know these parents love them. Donovan's question pondered the similarities between the issues she points out and those we face in trying to live as God's adopted children. Quoting Verrier, Donovan wrote in his e-mail:

> The issues all adoptees have "center around separation and loss, trust, rejection, guilt and shame, identity, intimacy, loyalty, and mastery or power and control."[7] The severing of the connection between the child and the one who gives life, identity, and security creates the *primal wound* which manifests itself "in a sense of loss, basic mistrust, anxiety, and depression, emotional and/or behavioral problems, and difficulties in relationships with significant others."[8]

He went on to explore our spiritual separation from the One who gave us life, identity, and security, the One with whom we were created to be "one"—a definite primal wound. He asks, "Aren't we like Adam and Eve, separated from the One who declared us to be 'very good,' and knowing that we are now 'not very good,' suffering from shame and fear that causes us to hide, even from God, just like they did?" He ended his e-mail by suggesting we let the cross deal with our primal wounds as well as our sins. The author of the letter to the Hebrews makes a similar suggestion.

📖 Read Hebrews 12:1–7 and 5:7–9. How did Jesus endure the cross? How does that help us to endure the suffering we face in this life?

_____

_____

_____

_____

Jesus always knew the love of His Father. He struggled in prayer to reconcile that fact with the suffering he faced. His question on the cross, "My God, my God, why have you forsaken me?" tells us He experienced the deep wound of separation that sin inflicts. Jesus endured by focusing on the joy set before Him of a bride cleansed and made beautiful for Him to enjoy for eternity. We are to endure, likewise, by fixing our eyes on Jesus. We are to consider Him, and know that the same love the Father had for His only begotten Son is now shed abroad in our hearts as adopted sons.

Often in our suffering we learn and know the love of the Father best. We would expect the good times to convince us of His love and care, but somehow it is in the struggles of life, when our hearts are broken open, that we become more receptive to His love.

APPLY Do you sometimes have difficulty in fully accepting, and being satisfied in the Father's love? What might be the reason for that?

_____

_____

_____

_____

How does fixing your eyes on Jesus, especially on the cross, help you endure in times of suffering?

_____

_____

_____

📖 Read Hebrews 12:8–11, 29. What is the purpose of discipline? How does it prove the love of the Father?

_____

_____

_____

Scotty Smith, the author of *The Reign of Grace* defines discipline as follows:

Discipline is God's loving commitment to mold his adopted children into the likeness of his only begotten Son. The grace of discipline is the various means by which the God of all grace administers his transforming discipline.[9]

Smith goes on to identify the means of grace including the hardship of suffering, the sting of rebuke, and the pain of punishment.

> Be trained by your hardships. Don't waste your suffering. Listen to the life-giving rebukes of your Father. Submit to his chastening. He loves you thoroughly. He loves you boldly.[10]

The last verse of chapter 12 tells us *"God is a consuming fire."* That's very scary, unless we know that He loves us, and the only thing He burns is our sin. He is perfecting us, preparing us to be part of the heavenly Jerusalem.

APPLY Are you ever tempted to think God must not love you if He has allowed suffering in your life? What is the logic behind that thought? What is the fallacy?

_____

_____

_____

_____

Can you remember a time when because of His discipline you experienced a deeper awareness of the Father's love?

_____

_____

_____

How has your community helped you in times of trial and fire?

_____

_____

_____

Read Hebrews 13:1–7. Why do you think Paul juxtaposes God's faithfulness and presence in our lives with his call to love and care within a community?

_____

_____

_____

As a community of faith we are responsible to live as if the Father really loves us. Let His perfect love cast out all our fear. Let us help one another through the suffering and discipline our loving Father brings into our lives. Let us encourage one another to fully accept and live in the knowledge that He loves us unconditionally. Let us open the door to our hearts and lives to generously share what the Lord has given us and taught us. Having our eyes open to the needs around us, our hearts open to care, and our voices ready to speak the truth are all ways we can *"let love of the brethren continue."*

The fact that He has promised to be with us gives us the courage to open our homes, remember the prisoners and persecuted, and challenge ourselves or our brothers and sisters caught in the traps of sexual immorality or materi-

---

Put Yourself in Their Shoes
DESIRING DISCIPLINE

I remember a day when my three-year-old daughter asked for a spanking. It wasn't the usual way children ask to be spanked by their deliberate disobedience. It was rather just a simple request. It baffled me until I realized what she really wanted was the loving embrace I always gave her after the discipline. Would that we have that same longing for our loving Father's embrace, to be willing to suffer whatever it takes to enable us to share in His holiness and feel His love in a deeper way.

"Let love of the brethren continue ... for He Himself has said, "I will never desert you, nor will I ever forsake you."
Hebrews 13:1,5

alism. A blind eye to the sins and sorrows of our brothers and sisters is failure to be community.

Verse 7 makes me think of how the church is, in a way, like foster care. Although we have been adopted, we are not yet physically seated at the right hand of our Father, enjoying the full benefits and security of our heavenly home. But we do have leaders who speak the Word of God to us and show us how to live by faith. Author Karen Mains points out how important a loving environment is to a new believer:

> Children brought into any world, whether it be of this earth or of the Spirit, will die if they are not nurtured in a loving home. It matters not where the fault lies. Too many evangelism efforts have remained unconcerned about their offspring, and too many churches have not experienced family to the degree that they were able to take care of their own offspring, let alone assume the responsibility for someone else's child. Evangelism without a functioning household of God will result in a high mortality rate.[11]

As you think back over this entire lesson and consider how you have partaken of the divine nature of knowledge, write a prayer that expresses the feelings you have.

_____

_____

_____

_____

_____

_____

_____

_____

_____

Our Loving Father, we praise You for revealing Yourself to us by Your Word, by Your Son, and by Your Spirit. We thank You for Your promise to never leave us or forsake us. We thank You that we do not have to fear for You are our helper, our covenant partner. We praise You that Your fire consumes only that which can be shaken—that which will not endure to the end of time. We praise You that even death cannot separate us from Your love.

Father we confess our failure to love others as You have loved us. Our love falls far short of the love of the incarnation. We so often fail to leave the comforts of our homes for even a short while. We fail to listen for Your voice, we don't seek to know Your ways, and so we don't always enter Your rest. Please forgive us, Lord.

We pray that by Your grace You would enable us to know You intimately. We pray that You would produce in us fruit that proves You have called us and are living in us. Please make our church a womb for disciple making. Give our community the grace to strengthen hands and knees, to heal the limbs and joints of our body, and to see that no one comes short of Your amazing grace. Help us all to be priests to one another.

Please protect us and deliver us from the evil one. We know he brings doubt, and fear, and shame to our minds in order to keep us from fully accepting Your love. We pray that our knowledge of You and of Your Son will strengthen our hearts to resist all his lies. Help us to stand firm together.

Works Cited

1. Paul Shattuck, one of the veteran missionaries leading Casa Yada.

2. Andrew Murray, *The Holiest of All* (New York: Fleming H. Revell, 1894 [13th reprinting, 1924]), 157.

3. Cyril Richardson, *Early Church Fathers* (New York, NY: Macmillan, 1970), 91–92.

4. Cyprian of Carthage, *The Unity of the Catholic Church*, trans. Maurice Bevenot (Westminster, MD: Newman, 1956; London: Longmans, Green and Co., 1957).

5. Robert Webber, *Ancient-Future Evangelism* (Grand Rapids, MI: Baker Books, 2003), 74.

6. Eugene Peterson, *A Long Obedience* (Downers Grove, IL: InterVarsity Press, 1980), 174–175.

7. Nancy Newton Verrier, *The Primal Wound* (Baltimore, MD: Gateway Press, Inc., 1997), 7.

8. Ibid., 21.

9. Scotty Smith, *The Reign of Grace* (West Monroe, LA: The Howard Publishing Co., 2003), 113.

10. Ibid., 116.

11. Karen Mains, *Open Heart, Open Home* (Elgin, IL: David C. Cook Co., 1976), 129.

Notes

5

Self-Control

One of the most well-developed discipleship communities I visited while researching for this study was Xenos Christian Fellowship in Columbus, Ohio. (*Xenos* is Greek for "sojourner in a foreign land.") Their fellowship consists of home churches led by men and women who have been trained in special classes for leadership development. Each home church has gender-specific cell groups for discipleship and encourages mentoring relationships among its members. In addition, many students who attend Ohio State University live together in ministry houses. Other singles live together in adult homes, and even some families share their lives in intentional community. Dennis McCallum, one of the senior pastors, explains their rationale:

> Home church planting depends on discipleship. This process of moving individuals from unbelief, self-centeredness, sin-dependency, and ignorance to a place of spiritual maturity takes years of patient investment, training, friendship and sacrifice. . . . In the early church they were "day by day" having meals together and meeting from house to house (Acts 2:46). This expression suggests Christian community took up a very large part of people's lives. Deep community like that described in the New Testament requires significant time investment into relationships.[1]

Active members at Xenos not only live in community, they are given many opportunities to be discipled or to disciple others.

Xenos . . .

. . . a community of self-control

Self-Control

DAY ONE

In a typical week during her college years, my friend Beth hung out with a girl she hoped to bring to Christ on Monday night, went to home church on Tuesday (hopefully bringing her friend along), took another class for leadership training on Wednesday, and met with a mentor on Thursday. She went to her cell group on alternating Friday nights so she could help out with the junior-high group every other week. On Saturday nights Beth might go to a party in her home church, and on Sunday she attended the Central Teaching at Xenos. She is married now and busy with her new career but still takes part in as many opportunities as she can, as her years of training helped her set priorities. No church leader said she had to do these things, but she saw the joy and fulfillment they brought to her friends and chose the committed lifestyle.

> The training needed to become competent as Christian leaders takes a great deal of time investment [and self-control]. Becoming a man or woman of God ready to lead a flock for Him will certainly interfere in a massive way with materialistic and entertainment pursuits that so dominate the schedules of adult Americans today. Like the rich young ruler, many American church members must turn away in sadness at the New Testament picture of radical Christian living.[2]

Someone who had visited a home church meeting at Xenos was surprised that I chose this church for my example of self-control. She said that many in the group she visited could not seem to control their tongues and began drinking and smoking as soon as the meeting ended. This legalistic understanding of self-control is just the opposite of what we will focus on in this chapter. Most likely, many attending the home church were not even believers yet, and those at Xenos let the Holy Spirit deal with specific sins in His own time. Rather, in their discipleship they emphasize truth and heart changes. I believe Xenos is an excellent example of self-control, or *egkrateia*, if this Greek word is defined as the dying to self that is necessary to partake of the divine nature and become fruitful servants in the kingdom of God. You can read more about Xenos at www.xenos.org.

SELF RESTRAINT: CHRIST'S EXAMPLE

The fruit of self-control is realizing we can't control our own human natures without the Holy Spirit's aid. In some ways, self-control means just the opposite of what our English translations imply. We cannot do it ourselves (omit *self*), and it is more relinquishment than it is control (omit *control*). The epistle to the Galatians explains that the work of the flesh is always in one of two directions—either to do evil, or to do good for credit. We need to be freed from sin, but also freed from our desires for accomplishment apart from the Holy Spirit. We can probably better understand the biblical idea of self-control if we call it *self-restraint*. In other words, we should say no to our selfish desires and allow the Holy Spirit to control us.

Before we explore what Paul taught the community of Galatia about this important concept we will see how Jesus showed us how to make room for the divine nature by living a life of *egkrateia*.

📖 Read Philippians 2:3–8. In what sense did Jesus say no to Himself? Why must we do the same?

_____
_____
_____

Jesus emptied Himself of His power and position as the second person of the Trinity and took the form of a human servant. Although we can never fully fathom this, He obviously died to self by deciding to look out for our interests and meet our needs. Likewise, to avoid living with selfishness and conceit, we need to look out for the interests or needs of others—self-denial for the purpose of love. This means we care more about others than about ourselves.

APPLY What does *"empty conceit"* look like in your life?

_____
_____
_____

📖 Read Matthew 4:1–4 and Deuteronomy 8:2–3. Compare the parallels between Jesus' situation in the wilderness and that of the people of Israel. Why do you think Jesus fasted for forty days?

_____
_____
_____
_____

Pastor and author John Piper in his excellent book *A Hunger for God* suggests the following:

[Jesus' fasting] was a voluntary act of identification with the people of God in their wilderness deprivation and trial. Jesus was saying in effect, "I have been sent to lead the people of God out of the bondage of sin into the Promised Land of salvation . . . Therefore I will take on the testing that they experienced. I will represent them in the wilderness and allow my heart to be probed with fasting to see where my allegiance is and who is my God. And, with the Spirit's help, I will triumph through this fasting. I will overcome the devil and lead all who trust me into the Promised Land of eternal glory."

Fasting tests where the heart is. And when it reveals that the heart is with God and not the world, a mighty blow is struck against Satan. For then Satan does not have a foothold.[3]

Jesus said no to the world, to His flesh, and to the devil when He fasted for forty days in the wilderness. Fasting helps us practice saying no to our flesh. This physical discipline can have amazing spiritual results.

APPLY What has been your experience with fasting?

_____
_____
_____
_____

2 PETER 1:3–7

"Seeing that His divine power has granted to us everything we need for life and godliness through the true knowledge of Him who called us . . . that you might become partakers of the divine nature. . . . For this reason bringing in with diligence supply in the faith of y'all the excellence and in excellence the knowledge and in knowledge the **self-control** *and in* **self-control** *the perseverance and in perseverance the godliness and in godliness the brotherly kindness and in brotherly kindness the love."*

(Author's Composite Translation)

📖 Read John 8:28–29; 12:49–50 and 14:10. How did Jesus display self-restraint?

_____

_____

_____

In the New American Standard Bible (NASB) the phrase "*on My own initiative*" is repeated in each of these passages from John. Satan first tempted Jesus to use His power as the Son of God to do something on His own initiative (Matthew 4:3). Living *"on every word that proceeds out of the mouth of God"* involves self restraint or waiting to hear from God before acting on our own initiatives.

APPLY How far should we take the idea of doing nothing on our own initiatives? How would it change the way we live?

_____

_____

_____

📖 Read Luke 9:21–24. What metaphors did Jesus use when he taught His disciples about self-control or self-restraint? If we could do this, how would our decision-making processes change?

_____

_____

_____

Denying self, taking up our crosses daily, and following Him are difficult metaphors to understand but even more difficult to practice. Besides saying no to ourselves, it means to embrace suffering just as He did for the glory of God. Our present evil age is all about avoiding pain, escaping suffering, and finding self-satisfaction. We often buy into this thinking because it feeds our flesh. But Jesus taught us to starve our flesh. He wants us to follow Him in suffering, being willing to experience rejection or even martyrdom. Jesus suffered so we could be delivered from this present evil age, not so we could enjoy materialistic abundance and freedom from pain.

APPLY How have you experienced denying self and taking up your cross?

_____

_____

_____

Self-Control

DAY TWO

SAYING NO TO THE FLESH

Paul opened his letter to the Galatians by recounting the story of his early years of discipleship. His purpose was to prove his apostleship and the truth of the gospel he preached. Consequently, he was eager to prove the difference between a human-centered and a God-centered gospel. Throughout his letter to the Galatian Christians, he contrasts the flesh and the Spirit. Today we will try to discern the differences. By doing so we hope to more fully understand the gift or fruit of self-control.

📖 Read Philippians 3:3–6. How does Paul describe himself before he met Christ? Compare and contrast his self-control before he became a believer to Christ's example of true self-control, which we studied the first day of this lesson. Then for added clarity, from your own experience of our society's view of self control, make a third category of secular or stoic ideas of self-control.

	Religious Self-Control	Christ's Self-Control	Stoic Self-Control
Center of Focus			
Empowerment			
Motive			
Action			
Result			

Hopefully, this exercise and your discussion of different ways of looking at self-control will help you understand how confusing this concept can be. Paul's description of his life as a Pharisee is a good example of religious self-control and finds parallels in all the major religions of this world. One of his purposes in writing the letter to the Galatians was to warn them against embracing a human-centered form of Christianity based on religious self-control. We need to distinguish the fleshly voices of legalism or self-directed discipline from the Spirit's still small voice calling us to love.

Like the Stoics of ancient Greece who used self-centered and self-empowering control, the strong-willed men and women of our culture discipline their bodies with extreme exercise or insane diets. Their examples may make us think we need to adopt their kind of self-control. Our schools, the media, and the huge focus on sports all hold up an ideal of self-control that is controlled by self. Personal mastery becomes the goal. Christ's gift of self-control is something quite different.

📖 Read the only verses in the New Testament that use *egkrateia*: Acts 24:25; Galatians 5:23; and 2 Peter 1:6. See its adjective form in Titus 1:8 and once in its noun form, referring to athletes in 1 Corinthians 9:25.

Word Study
FLESH

The Greek word *sarx*, translated as "flesh" in the New Testament, denotes the fleshy part of the body, or the whole body. . . . it may mean the whole man . . . or the earthly part of man. In Galatians Paul uses it to denote the whole personality of man as going in the wrong direction, as directed to earthly pursuits rather than the service of God. The man whose horizon is limited by the flesh is by that very fact opposed to God. He lives "after the flesh," that flesh that "lusts against the Spirit."

Source: L. L. Morris, *The New Bible Dictionary* (Grand Rapids, MI: Eerdmans Publishing Co., 1976), 411.

Did You Know?
DEALING WITH SINFUL NATURE

All flesh is sinful, but our sin can go in dissimilar directions. Because everyone's flesh is different in some ways, we don't all have the same temptations. Some of us need books like Richard Foster's *Celebration of Discipline* because our flesh is weak and lazy. But others, who can read the Bible through in a year and have no trouble fasting, and love to read books about discipline may need to deal with a flesh full of pride. If we are there, we need to realize our flesh loves discipline and we need to learn more Spirit control. Hopefully, this lesson will help you identify the ways your flesh tries to trick you into saying yes to its desires.

Why do you think the writers of the New Testament say so little about self-control when both the culture in Jesus' time and in our day emphasize it so much?

_____

_____

_____

The *Theological Dictionary of the New Testament* offers the following explanation:

> It is significant that biblical religion finds so little place for the concept of *egkrateia* which in the Hellenistic and Greek world is so [emphasized]. The reason for this is that biblical man regarded his life as determined and directed by the command of God. There was thus no place for the self-mastery which had a large place in autonomous ethics.[4]

The apostles' limited use of the word and their redefining it as a fruit of the Spirit clarifies its Christian meaning. In some ways it directly contrasts its common Greek meaning and the way self-control is used and understood in our culture today.

APPLY Why do you think your flesh likes and wants control? How and when do you say no to that?

_____

_____

_____

📖 Read Galatians 2:18–21. What was Paul's solution to his struggle with his flesh?

_____

_____

_____

Part of Paul's crucifixion with Christ was his death to the law, or the tearing down of what his flesh had built: a man-centered religion that focused on a rigid keeping of the rules. Our flesh likes that kind of religion because it gives us a sense of control and pride. But the gospel message is that Christ not only died for our forgiveness, but wants to live in us. Although we still live in the flesh, our flesh does not rule us, Christ does. Our part is to live by faith. That means we learn to say no to our flesh and yes to Christ. By faith we embrace Christ's love for us, we are enabled by God's grace working in us, and we celebrate the freedom of life in the Spirit.

APPLY What are the most common battlegrounds for the war between your flesh and the Spirit? Are you more likely to be tempted by the evident works of the flesh or the more hidden fleshly desires for control and pride?

_____

_____

_____

"The fruit of the Spirit is . . . self-control."

Galatians 5:23

📖 Read Galatians 5:19–21 and 24. What are some things our flesh wants that we need to say no to? Were you surprised or convicted by any of them? What should we do with our fleshly passions and desires?

_____

_____

_____

_____

Those works of the flesh that have not yet been crucified in us convict us. Christ's work in us always brings us to the cross. He changes us, cleanses us, frees us, and prepares us for glory.

Author Dallas Willard writes about our part in the crucifixion of our flesh:

> Our part in this transformation, in addition to constant faith and hope in Christ, is purposeful, strategic use of our bodies in ways which will retrain them, replacing "the motions of sin in our members" with the motions of Christ. This is how we take up our cross daily. It is how we submit our bodies a living sacrifice, how we "offer the parts of our body to Him as instruments of righteousness" (Rom. 6:13).[5]

APPLY How can and does your community help you to say no to the flesh?

_____

_____

_____

SAYING NO TO LEGALISM

Self-Control

DAY THREE

Paul wrote to the Galatians to warn young Christians about the danger of giving up their liberty and going back into bondage. Jewish converts in Galatia tried to convince these Gentile converts that they should keep the Jewish law in order to be good Christians. Paul, however, showed them that Christ had freed them not only from the bondage of sin but also from bondage to the law. They could not generate a relationship or credit with God by keeping the law apart from Christ.

📖 Read Galatians 1:6–10 and 3:1–3. What perversion of the gospel do you think Paul is referring to? Why is legalism attractive to our flesh?

_____

_____

_____

The foolish Galatians had been tricked into thinking that the beginning of their salvation was the work of the Spirit, but that their spiritual growth toward perfection was their own responsibility. They thought they needed to keep the rules to become better Christians. Even though this would have no bearing on how God saw them, it could impress others. Our flesh seeks human approval. If we can show others how godly we are by keeping rules, we think we are better Christians. Our flesh likes that. With legalism self is in control, but it is not under control. Those are two different things.

APPLY How do you know if you are trying to be perfected by the flesh or if you are trusting Christ to perfect you?

_____

_____

_____

📖 Read Galatians 3:10–14. How does Paul explain why legalism or doing the works of the law does not bring us to salvation?

_____

_____

_____

GALATIANS 3:10–11

"Anyone who tries to live by his own effort, independent of God, is doomed to failure. Scripture backs this up: 'Utterly cursed is every person who fails to carry out every detail written in the Book of the law.' The obvious impossibility of carrying out such a moral program should make it plain that no one can sustain a relationship with God that way. The person who lives in right relationship with God does it by embracing what God arranges for him. Doing things for God is the opposite of entering into what God does for you."

(The Message)

In his translation (_The Message_) Eugene Peterson captures the essence of Paul's argument in these verses. Paul's point is that self-effort, or a false understanding of self-control, will lead to failure, or even more graphically, to the curse of death. Such dire talk should make those with legalistic mind-sets rather fearful. Peterson goes on in his rendering of verse 12 to say, "Rule keeping does not naturally evolve into living by faith, but only perpetuates itself in more and more rule keeping." God starts His work in our hearts, and our obedience is the fruit of that work. That is what living by faith is. We are to enter into what God does for us and partake of His nature. We are to deny ourselves, even the self that wants to do the works of the law apart from faith.

APPLY Have you ever been in a legalistic church? How did that affect your Christian growth?

_____

_____

_____

📖 Read Galatians 3: 21–25. What is the purpose of the law?

_____

_____

_____

Extra Mile
BY FAITH

Count how many times Paul uses the word _faith_ in Galatians 3. He must have forgotten his composition professor's warning to not repeat the same word so many times in a paragraph. But there is no other word he could use, because there is no other way. We must learn to live by faith.

The law was a guardian for God's people before Christ came. It helped them see their need for Him. It revealed to them how impossible it was to keep and showed them their need of a Savior. Its purpose was, then and now, to get us moving in the direction of Christ. But once He was revealed, He made it clear that we can only be justified by faith in Him.

We should read the Ten Commandments and the Beatitudes as God's intentions for us. They bring us to conviction, repentance, and complete dependence on Him. Only then can we trust the Holy Spirit to fulfill them in and through us, based on the finished work of Christ. _Egkrateia_ helps us to say no to the idea that our flesh can use the law to make points with God. It has never worked that way, and never will.

APPLY Why is repentance more important than discipline? How will changing your efforts from doing certain things to knowing Christ more affect your personal growth and community life?

_____

_____

_____

_____

📖 Read Galatians 5:22–23. Why is it important to see self-restraint as a fruit of the Spirit? What wrong ideas come to mind if we think of *egkrateia* as self-control rather than giving up our control? What happens when we try to control ourselves apart from the Spirit's work?

_____

_____

_____

_____

The only way we can control self or our flesh is to put it under the Spirit's control. John Sanderson writes:

> There is a sort of self-control which can reject a particular sinful act; but if that self-control refuses the grace of God, the result is really only trading one sin for another, and the latter will be worse than the former. Thus does Jesus rebuke preaching which is negative only, a preaching which calls on people to give up this or that evil habit but never confronts the sinner with Jesus Christ and His claims. We must not be taken in by the artificial fruit; we must seek for that self-control which is the gift of God.[6]

Refusing the grace of God means to think we can do it ourselves, rather than depending on the power of the Holy Spirit. Some churches teach self-control and self-discipline with more emphasis on obedience than on grace. By grace I mean not just that God forgives and cleanses us, but that He gives us the power to obey. He gives us the Holy Spirit. When pastors do not preach grace, people try hard to obey by self-control and self-discipline. They soon fall into the trap of legalism and pride. True self-control must be the fruit of the Holy Spirit.

SAYING NO TO PRIDE AND PREJUDICE

O n Day 2 we focused on the more evident works of the flesh and yesterday on the ugly sin of legalism. In the verses we study today, Paul helps us focus on the twin sins of pride and prejudice. We will see how it takes both the Spirit's control and the unity of the body of Christ to root out these heinous sins.

📖 Read Galatians 3:25–29. Why does our flesh want to emphasize differences between us and others who are not like us? How and why do we say no to prejudice when we are in Christ?

_____

_____

_____

One of the best books I have read on the topic of prejudice and how it can be overcome in our lives is *The Beloved Community* by Charles Marsh. He records the history of the civil rights movement and the work Christ has done in His church in the past fifty years to bring about racial reconciliation. He took his title from Martin Luther King's description and passion for beloved community.

> Beloved community was the realization of divine love in lived social relation. . . . It was the passion to make human life and social existence a parable of God's love for the world. It was *agape*: the outrageous venture of loving the other without conditions—a risk and a costly sacrifice.[7]

This reminds me of the bigger picture of our study of 2 Peter 1. The reason we are to partake of *egkrateia* (and all the other gifts in our list) is to ultimately bring us to love. We will never have a loving community unless we allow the Spirit to deal with our prejudices.

These verses in Galatians describe the truth that brings an end to prejudice. By faith we are children of God—we share the same family. We are all clothed in Christ—we share the same covering. We are all one in Christ—we share the same body. We are all heirs according to promise—we share the same future. In Christ, prejudice is abolished.

> No longer is the church solely in the business of saving individual souls from damnation, but it embodies the "great event" of the cross by making free space for redemptive community . . . the reconciling church demonstrates to the world that "it is still true that in Christ there is neither Jew nor Gentile (Negro or white) and that out of one blood God made all men to dwell upon the face of the earth."[8]

Even though Christ has made us one, we don't always have the eyes of faith to see it. We still misunderstand and fear those who look different. Marsh explores some ways the Spirit has helped communities overcome this. He quotes Clarence Jordan of Koinonia Farms in Georgia:

> If the barriers that divide man, and cause wars, race conflict, economic competition, class struggle, labor disputes are ever to be broken down they must be broken down in small groups of people living side by side, who plan consciously and deliberately to find a way wherein they can all contribute to the kingdom according to their respective abilities.[9]

Author Peter Scazzero in his book, *The Emotionally Healthy Church,* describes a similar approach in what he calls "incarnational living."

> When we choose to incarnate, we hang between our own world and the world of another person. We are called to remain faithful to who we are, not losing our essence, while at the same time entering into the world of another. We can be assured, however, that as Jesus' incarnation and death brought great life, so our choice to do the same will also result in resurrection life and much fruit in us and others. . . . When we go out of ourselves and live briefly in the world of another person, we never return to our own lives the same person. God changes us into the image of His Son through the process.[10]

Prejudice is overcome when we live side by side, when we enter the world of others, when we seek to really understand and appreciate the gifts and parts they play in the body of Christ. The Spirit uses small mixed groups and incarnation to help us partake of beloved community and overcome a history of suspicion, fear, and hurt.

 How have you personally experienced either prejudice or beloved community?

_____

_____

What do you think of living incarnationally? What would keep you from moving in that direction?

_____

_____

_____

📖 Read Galatians 5:13–16, 26. How does Paul contrast life in the Spirit and life in the flesh in these verses? How is conflict resolved?

_____

_____

_____

_____

When we partake of *egkrateia*, we allow the Spirit to not only control us but to fill us with His love. When we can say no to the flesh and its temptation to conflict, pride, provoking others, and envy, we learn to love and serve one another.

Tara Barthel and Judy Dabler in their book *Peacemaking Women* give excellent teaching and many examples of how the Spirit leads us in conflict resolution. Tara and Judy write:

> In order to experience peace in the church, we are also called to clothe ourselves with the virtues that God graciously endows to us. Although we are growing in Christ, we are not yet perfect. Within the intimate boundaries of our church family, we will bump one another and sparks will fly. That is why we have been called to bear with one another in love. . . . Without affection and compassion, we will have no hope of forgiving one another's inevitable failings and offenses. Genuine Christian fellowship begins when we let one another down, become disillusioned, but still choose to forgive and forbear.[11]

 How have conflicts in the church been handled in your experience? What can we learn from both good and bad examples?

_____

_____

_____

When we partake of Christ's self-control, we allow the Spirit to not only control us but to fill us with His love.

> **"Bear one another's burdens, and thus fulfill the law of Christ. . . . But let each examine his own work and then he will have reason for boasting in regard to himself alone and not in regard to another. For each one shall bear his own load."**
>
> **Galatians 6:2, 4–5**

📖 Read Galatians 6:1–5. What do you think Paul means by those who are *"spiritual"*? How does Paul describe a life that fulfills *"the law of Christ"*? What implications do you find in these verses about community life?

_____

_____

_____

_____

I think the phrase *"you who are spiritual"* in verse 1 refers back to the people Paul describes in the previous chapter as those who walk by the Spirit. He points out that when we seek to restore a brother caught in sin, we must be under the control of the Spirit. Our flesh is so tempted to come to a brother like this in pride. But in order to bear other's burdens, we must see our own weaknesses, and know that we need the Spirit more than ever.

I wonder if Paul intentionally included the seemingly contradictory statements regarding bearing others burdens and each one bearing his own load in order to show how community life must always include both corporate and individual responsibilities. We are to truly care for others, but each individual must also realize that he or she is responsible before God to walk in humility, to work faithfully, and to do their own part.

 Share an incident where someone expected the community to go beyond the boundaries of corporate responsibility to carry too much of one person's load? Why might that be dangerous to both the individual and the community?

_____

_____

_____

_____

Self-Control

DAY FIVE

SAYING YES TO THE SPIRIT

I lived through the glorious and sometimes divisive charismatic renewal in the 1970s. For many of us, it was an amazing time of saying yes to the Spirit in new and exciting ways. But disagreements over exactly how the Spirit worked, which gifts were for whom, and what manifestations were real left many of us confused and sorrowful as we saw our churches dividing. Thankfully, most of us have agreed to disagree on the less-important questions and have focused in on the simple fact that we must all say yes to the Spirit. Those things that fed our flesh and pride were eventually flushed away by the Spirit's gentle work in us all. Knowing that you might interpret controversial verses in today's study differently than I do, my questions will be more generic, but I challenge us all to open ourselves up to the Spirit in whatever ways He would lead us in this lesson.

📖 Read Galatians 3:13–14 and 4:6–7. Why did Christ die according to these verses? Why does God send His Spirit? How are we brought into the relationship of the Trinity?

_____

_____

_____

We usually think the answer to this first question is to save us and make a way for us to go to heaven. Paul's answer, however, broadens the scope of God's purposes. Christ redeemed us from the curse in order that we might receive the Holy Spirit. My pastor, Michael Kelly, recently said, "Jesus' entire ministry was making a way for the Holy Spirit to come to you—to prepare you as a vessel for the Holy Spirit. . . . The essence, the central component, the epicenter of Christian life is the Holy Spirit."

Since God has adopted us as His children, He has sent forth His Spirit into our hearts to draw us into the intimate relationship of the Trinity. We not only become heirs of future glory but partakers of present communion. We can call God our Abba—"Daddy." And, as we shall see in the remaining verses, this enables us to walk with Him, talk with Him, follow Him, and to live in vital fellowship with Him and with our brothers and sisters.

APPLY How does knowing that Christ died that you might be filled with the Spirit make a difference in how you pray and what you pray for?

_____

_____

_____

📖 Read Galatians 5:4–6 and Romans 13:10. What is the _"only thing that counts"_ (NIV) in Christianity? What examples of _"faith working through love"_ (NASB) can you think of? What part does the Spirit have in all this?

_____

_____

_____

_____

Since God is love, His Spirit convicts us of those things that keep us from love and enables us to become conduits of His love. When we try to do anything apart from the Holy Spirit, even good things like keeping the law, it is the work of the flesh and so is outside the realm of grace. It is not going to count. Waiting by faith for the hope of righteousness is anticipating the Holy Spirit's guidance, believing He will show us His will, knowing He will give us everything we need for life and godliness, relying on His power, depending on His grace, and being filled with His love. What He does in us and through us will always be expressed in love. The work of the Holy Spirit is to make faith real and relational.

 APPLY Think of several examples of times when your faith expressed itself through love. Can you share that with your community without pride?

> _"The only thing that counts is faith expressing itself through love."_
>
> **_Galatians 5:6 (NIV)_**

_____

_____

_____

_____

📖 Read Galatians 5:16–18, 22–25. How do we live by the Spirit and walk
by the Spirit?

_____

_____

_____

I believe Paul's phrase *"live by the Spirit"* refers back to Galatians 2 and 3
where he talks about justification by faith and receiving the Spirit by hear-
ing with faith. The Spirit of God gives us new life. We are born again by the
Spirit when He gives us new life, and we *"walk by the Spirit"* in the present.
Walking refers to our lives today, what we do and say, where we go, what
choices we make. All of this must be led and enabled by the Spirit. Just as
Jesus did nothing on His own initiative, so we are to do nothing without the
Holy Spirit. We must not only say "no" to the flesh, we must say "yes" to the
Spirit. The fruit of doing so is love.

 Where does your imagination go if you think of *walking __by__* in
terms of next to, moving with, alongside, in the presence of, in
union with? Does that help you put feet to the idea of walking by
the Spirit?

_____

_____

_____

📖 Read Galatians 6:7–10. How do we sow to the Spirit? What is the difference between the *"doing good"* mentioned in these verses and trying
to be good by keeping the law?

_____

_____

_____

The difference between sowing to the flesh and sowing to the Spirit is made
manifest by the lists Paul gave us in chapter 5. But he doesn't say exactly
how we do it. Since we are studying self-control, I wonder if different kinds
of sowing are determined by who is in control. Are we in control of our
lives, or have we handed over the control to the Holy Spirit? Who is win-
ning the battle in our inner beings? Are we partaking of the divine nature
of *egkrateia*? The good deeds might look the same, but we usually can know,
and God knows for sure if we are sowing to the flesh or to the Spirit. Losing
heart and growing weary might be signs that we are doing it in our flesh.
The Spirit, on the other hand, never grows weary and takes every opportunity to show love, especially to those in the community of faith.

 How does the quote from my pastor in the sidebar make you feel?
In what ways might it help you to say "Yes" to the Holy Spirit?

> **"The Holy Spirit is a fighter. He is tenacious, rude, abrupt, and con-flict-oriented when it comes to our flesh. He will not facilitate our love of self. He will always fight against our idols and addic-tions."**
>
> **Michael Kelly**

_____

_____

_____

_____

Please pray with me and write a prayer of your own that focuses on the things in your life that the Spirit wants to deal with today.

_____

_____

_____

_____

_____

_____

_____

_____

_____

Father, we praise You for Your sovereignty. You are indeed in control of all things. May we ever submit to that control and find rest in Your loving care and guidance. Christ, we praise You for Your willingness to empty Yourself, to take on the form of a bond-servant, to humbly submit to the cross that we might receive the Holy Spirit. Holy Spirit, we praise You for making the divine nature available to us, and helping us to partake of it together. Thank You for the fruit You are producing in us. Thank You, Lord, for giving us to one another. We know and understand why it is impossible to live the Christian life alone.

Father, we confess that too often we walk alone. We are not open to the Holy Spirit's control in our lives. We are not mindful of His presence. We do not rely on His power. We are not aware of His still small voice. We are too distracted by our flesh, the world, and the enemy's lies. We don't take the time to be quiet before You. We don't take enough time to be with Your people and hear what You have to say through them. We don't hear You speaking to us through Your Word when we fail to read and meditate on it. Please forgive us and cleanse us.

Father, we pray that You would enable us to die to self, take up our cross, and follow You. We pray for those in the midst of the battle right now. Convince them to partake of the divine nature of *egkrateia*. Cause them to know their need of both the body of Christ and the Spirit of Christ. We pray, too, for those in the desert, experiencing the loneliness of solitary confinement. May they be open to what You must teach them there, and bring them back to us soon.

Deliver us, Lord, from the rule of our flesh. Help us to say no to sexual immorality, idolatry, strife, anger, factions, and envy. Identify and convict us of any legalism, pride, or prejudice still clinging to our flesh. Enable us, O God, to love You with all our hearts and to love one another with a self-sacrificing love. And we will give You all praise, honor, and glory forever. Amen.

1. Dennis McCallum, "Urban Home Church Planting at Xenos," www.xenos.org.

2. Ibid.

3. John Piper, *A Hunger for God* (Wheaton, IL: Crossway Books, 1997), 57, 58.

4. G. Kittle, editor, *Theological Dictionary of the New Testament*, vol. 2 (Grand Rapids, MI: Eerdmans, 1964), 342.

5. Dallas Willard, "The Spirit Is Willing—The Body as a Tool for Spiritual Growth" in *The Christian Educator's Handbook on Spiritual Formation* (Wheaton, IL: Victor Books, 1994), 229.

6. John Sanderson, *The Fruit of the Spirit* (Phillipsburg, NJ: P and R Publishing, 1985), 137.

7. Charles Marsh, *The Beloved Community* (New York, NY: Basic Books, 2005), 2.

8. Ibid, 45.

9. Ibid, 84.

10. Peter Scazzero, *The Emotionally Healthy Church* (Grand Rapids, MI: Zondervan, 2003), 189, 191.

11. Tara Barthel and Judy Dabler, *Peace Making Women* (Grand Rapids MI: Baker Books, 2005).

6

Perseverance

"**P**risons are a wonderful place for community!" My mother's cousin, George Soltau, made this surprising statement while telling me of his experiences with a prison ministry started by Chuck Colson. In the late 1970s, the Lord led George to help Prison Fellowship establish small-group ministries in prisons. Convinced that the small group was God's way of growing people, he found it especially effective where prisoners lived together and had plenty of time to consider the claims of Christ. Many were open to the truth of the gospel and in their groups they established new kinds of relationships they had never experienced before.

George adopted Ephesians 6:10 as his key verse: *"Finally, be strong in the Lord, and in the strength of His might."* Written by an *"ambassador in chains,"* these words became George's challenge to the men and women who joined the fellowship of Christian prisoners all over the world. Just as we are learning to partake of the divine nature in community, the small groups in Prison Fellowship learned to take up the divine armor of God so they could live and persevere in His strength.

As each group formed, everyone shared their stories. They told about lives devoid of love and affirmation, of hard times, negative experiences, and feelings of worthlessness. The gospel of God's love for them, manifested by the life of Christ, through the work of the Holy Spirit, turned their stories around. The small groups helped each one identify the gifts and strengths

Prison Fellowship

. . . a community of perseverance.

"Perseverance [*hupomone*] is a remaining under, steadfastness, constancy, a patient waiting for . . . that calm and unruffled temper with which a good man bears the evils of life, whether they proceed from persons or things. It also manifests itself in a sweet submission to the providential appointments of God and fortitude in the presence of the duties and conflicts of life."

Source: E. McChesney, *The New Unger's Bible Dictionary* (Chicago, IL: Moody Press, 1966) 396.

Perseverance

DAY ONE

2 PETER 1:3–7

*"Seeing that His divine power has granted to us everything we need for life and godliness through the true knowledge of Him who called us . . . that you might become partakers of the divine nature. . . . For this reason bringing in with diligence supply in the faith of y'all the excellence and in excellence the knowledge and in knowledge the self-control and in self-control the **perseverance** and in **perseverance** the godliness and in godliness the brotherly kindness and in brotherly kindness the love."*

(Author's Composite Translation)

Christ had given them. Over the years, they were amazed to see the results of acceptance, forgiveness, love, and affirmation in the lives of countless inmates, guards, wardens, and staff personnel. They found that perseverance in difficult places like prisons takes two important ingredients: knowing you are loved and knowing you can stand strong in the Lord's strength. The communities formed by Prison Fellowship provided this for many. The sad part was the fact that so few churches on the outside were healthy enough to accept and love the inmates when they got out of prison.

Uncle George has passed away now, but Prison Fellowship continues on with a similar ministry called the *InnerChange Freedom Initiative*. This ministry involves pastors and churches in the small-group ministry so prisoners can continue these relationships when they are released from prison. You can read more about it at www.pfm.org. The following is a quote from that site.

> The InnerChange Freedom Initiative is different from other rehabilitative programs. We consider IFI a transformational model, not therapeutic, although IFI is like a therapeutic community in many ways. Both types of programs operate through small groups and seek to equip members for life after prison.

The transformational model seeks to restore the inmate to God first, then builds on this new relationship to recast human relationships. Through support groups and classes, IFI connects inmates with a loving community of like-minded people to encourage and affirm them.

DIVINE PERSEVERANCE

Although we have many examples in the Gospels of how Christ persevered, Paul in his letter to the community at Rome makes more references to God the Father's Perseverance. So instead of seeing how Christ revealed this quality, we will look through the eyes of Paul at how the Father and the whole Trinity have persevered with mankind since the beginning of time.

📖 Read Romans 1:1–6 and Isaiah 42:1–4. How do these verses describe the perseverance of God?

_____

_____

_____

God not only planned, promised, and prophesied the way He would redeem this fallen world and His chosen ones, but also He is patiently carrying it all to completion. Did you notice in the Isaiah passage the Trinity's working together to reestablish justice in this world? We have fallen so low and in so many ways that it takes God's perseverance to bring about our redemption.

📖 Read Romans 2:4–8. In what way does God's kindness, tolerance, and patience (perseverance) lead us to repentance? What does it mean to *"think lightly"* of something? How can we make our thoughts heavier? How does that help us to persevere?

_____

_____

_____

_____

Spend some time in your study group or community encouraging one another by stories of God's kindness in your individual or corporate lives. Remind each other of the goodness and forgiveness of God. Talk about what led up to the last time you truly repented. How did God's kindness, forbearance, and patience factor into it? Study the Perseverance Cycle chart below and help one another identify the cycle of how God's perseverance leads to our repentance, and then as we learn to partake of His perseverance it leads to good works.

GOD'S
PERSEVERANCE

REPENTANCE   **PERSEVERANCE**   GOOD WORKS
                 CYCLE

OUR
PERSEVERANCE

APPLY   How has God's perseverance led you to repentance?

_____

_____

📖 Read Romans 3:21–26. What do these verses tell us about the forbearance of God?

_____

_____

God's forbearance or tolerance is part of His perseverance. It means holding back wrath with long-suffering and patience as He waits for fruit to grow in our lives. His plan is for the righteousness of Christ to bear fruit in us who believe. It is His way of being just but also justifying us and bringing glory to His name.

APPLY   Why does the righteousness of God being manifested in us require His perseverance?

_____

_____

_____

_____

"Being justified as a gift by His grace through the redemption which is in Christ Jesus. . . . This was to demonstrate His righteousness, because in the forbearance of God He passed over the sins previously committed . . . that He might be just and the justifier of the one who has faith in Jesus."

Romans 3:24–26

📖 Read Romans 15:5–7. In the literal Greek, verse 5 reads, "*May the God of perseverance and encouragement grant you a spirit of unity.*" What would this imply concerning both the perseverance of God and the fact that we can partake of that perseverance? What does that lead to?

_____

_____

_____

Because He is a God of perseverance and encouragement, He gives that to us so we can be of the same mind and of one voice in our praise to Him. Notice how perseverance carries us closer to community, to each other, and to God's love. All this is for the purpose of glorifying God.

APPLY What do you see in your community that has come about through the perseverance and encouragement of God?

_____

_____

_____

Perseverance presupposes a perspective that partakes of God's promises.

KEYS TO PERSEVERANCE

Steadfastness and constancy can only be formed in us by keeping our eyes on Christ and our hearts open to the gifts He wants to give us. The reason we need to partake of self-restraint before we can open the gift of perseverance is that it has trained us to say no to ourselves and yes to the Spirit. Restraint allows us to receive. And when it comes to persevering in our daily walk, especially when it involves suffering and tribulation, we need to receive all the help we can get.

By way of warning, today you will be reading and studying a long passage that is somewhat difficult to understand. (You will need to persevere.) Instead of trying to understand each phrase and picking apart every particular idea Paul presents, try to understand his overall argument and how he is training us to persevere in our suffering and struggle against sin.

📖 Read Romans 5:1–3, 17, 21. How is grace involved in perseverance?

_____

_____

_____

In the first four chapters of his letter to the Romans, Paul shows how God has brought about our justification through perseverance. We, by faith, simply receive the gift of salvation and find peace with God through Christ. Then in chapters 5 and 6, Paul gives key perspectives that will enable us to persevere. The first key is found in a phrase in verse 2: *"this grace in which we stand."* Remember, grace is the ability God gives us to obey Him, follow

Him, and partake of all His gifts. In order to persevere, we must stand in grace. We must be open to and receive the abundance of grace. Indeed, grace must reign in us. Without it we cannot persevere.

APPLY How does Satan minimize grace in by convincing believers it is nothing more than mercy and forgiveness? Why?

_____

_____

_____

📖 Read Romans 5:3–5. Paul says we know that tribulation or suffering brings about perseverance—how do you think we know that? Why is that a given? What does the Holy Spirit have to do with it?

_____

_____

_____

Here is the second key perspective: we are to exult in our sufferings. We find joy in suffering when we see it as a training ground for perseverance. Depending on our perspectives, we can respond to suffering either with bitterness and despair, or with joy and hope. If, in our times of suffering, we see only our pain and turn our backs on God, we will obviously not learn to persevere. But the Holy Spirit will not allow us to do that for long. He is there with us, pouring God's love into our hearts.

Some Christians read these verses and decide the only way they can persevere is through denial. They pretend there is no pain in their tribulation, and they call their denial faith. They always wear big smiles on their faces and think it is exaltation. But they only fool themselves, and by these false choices fail to partake of the gift of true perseverance. The psalms of lament teach us to walk through pain, being honest about it, but keeping our face toward God. Always remember, the comfort of His love will outlast the suffering.

APPLY In what ways have you tried to persevere through trials without really trusting in God's grace? How did that work?

_____

_____

_____

📖 Read Romans 6:1–7. What does it mean to be baptized into Christ's death? How can that enable us to persevere? What does it mean to _"walk in newness of life"_? How would believing we are freed from sin contribute to our persevering against it?

_____

_____

_____

_____

The sacrament of water baptism symbolizes our union with Christ in His death and resurrection. The sacrament of the Lord's Supper is the ongoing rite of participation in His death (see 1 Corinthians 10:16). Both of these sacraments help us to grasp the importance of being united with Christ in His death. We persevere in life by realizing our death to sin. This is only accomplished by the mysterious union with Christ in His death. By His blood, the power of sin over us is broken. I can persevere in a life of righteousness because I have been freed from sin's reign. In the words of Lesslie Newbigin:

> Personal commitment to Jesus Christ [is] continually renewed through a continually repeated re-incorporation into His dying and His resurrection.[1]

The keys to perseverance are to stand in grace, to find joy in suffering, to continually re-incorporate ourselves into Christ's death, to believe the right things, and to continue yielding.

📖 Read Romans 6:8–11. Why is our mindset so important to perseverance? What are we to believe, know, and consider?

_____

_____

_____

We don't persevere by sheer will-power; we persevere by believing the right things. We must believe we can live in resurrection power. We must know that Christ's death conquered death and sin, then consider ourselves dead to sin and alive to God in Christ. Perseverance is maintained and accomplished in the battle for our minds. Satan wants us to think that we persevere by our own personal struggles to do the right thing. Paul tells us that our part is to believe the right things, and Christ will accomplish "the doing" through His dwelling in us. We live by grace, through faith.

APPLY Do you agree that what you believe is more important than what you do? Why?

_____

_____

_____

How can we remind one another in our community of the things we need to believe, know, and consider?

_____

_____

📖 Read Romans 6:12–18. Why does Paul say, _"go on presenting"_ or _"continue yielding"_? What does that have to do with perseverance? Do you think believing we are _"under grace"_ is a fact we accept once, or something we need to practice believing every day of our lives? How does forgetting we are under grace lead to giving up?

_____

_____

_____

KEYS TO PERSEVERANCE:

- Stand in grace
- Find joy in suffering
- Continually re-incorporate into Christ's death
- Believe the right things
- Continually yield

How to persevere: We don't persevere by sheer will-power; we persevere by believing the right things.

We may think perseverance is something we have to do rather than a gift we are invited to receive and partake of. We try to fix ourselves or our painful situations rather than simply yielding to God in the midst of our struggles. We would rather deny the problem, get around it, defend it, figure it out, or conquer it—anything but simple yielding. If we make grace a place of abiding and see our part as continually yielding, Christ will deal with sin and death (and all that accompany them). We simply live in His grace, moment by moment, day by day. Our focus is not on trying to be like Him in our own strength, but being open and receptive to His voice, His leading, His directions, His gifts, and His strength. He will give us the grace to persevere when we *"go on presenting"* ourselves to Him.

APPLY What happens in your life when you forget you are under grace?

_____

_____

_____

Has your view of baptism and the Lord's Supper changed as a result of this study? If so, in what ways?

_____

_____

_____

WAITING WITH HOPE

Perseverance
DAY THREE

I used to think it would be wonderful to hear from God directly like Abraham did, until I realized that it would sometimes be twenty years in between God's visits. Abraham's faith during those silent years was remarkable. He didn't have the Word of God like we do, the Holy Spirit living within him, or a community of faith surrounding him. He just had a promise. In Romans 4:18, Paul tells us that Abraham believed in *"hope against hope."* I find that an intriguing phrase and wonder what it means. I am sure it has something to do with perseverance. *The Message* says, *"When everything was hopeless, Abraham believed anyway."* Perseverance goes "hand in hand" with both hope and waiting.

📖 Read Romans 8:12–15. How does knowing we are adopted help us to persevere?

_____

_____

_____

In Lesson 5, we learned to partake of the divine nature of knowledge. Just as the Father, Son, and Spirit know one another, we can know them and their love. We are part of the divine family. Knowing that we are adopted should diminish our fear. Fear and hopelessness threaten endurance. On the other hand, "hope against hope," or a firm hold on God's promises,

📖 **Doctrine**
HOPE

"[Those who] truly believe in the Lord Jesus . . . may, in this life, be certainly assured that they are in the state of grace, and may rejoice in the hope of the glory of God; which hope shall never make them ashamed. This certainty is not a bare conjectural and probable persuasion, grounded upon a fallible hope; but an infallible assurance of faith, founded upon the divine truth of the promises of salvation, the inward evidence of those graces unto which these promises are made, [and] the testimony of the Spirit of adoption witnessing with our spirits that we are the children of God."

Source: *The Westminster Confession of Faith*, Chapter 18

strengthens our perseverance. Knowing the Father as our "Abba," the Spirit as our guide, and Christ as our brother enables us to say no to our flesh and yes to God.

 What do you think it means to *"hope against hope"*? Give an example.

_____

_____

_____

_____

📖 Read Romans 8:16. How have you experienced the truth of this verse in your own life? How has that helped you persevere?

_____

_____

_____

When I asked this question of a friend who works with abused children, she thought of Psalm 68:6 where it says, *"God sets the lonely in families"* (NIV). Some of her clients have been taken from their natural parents and are waiting to be adopted. One of their greatest fears, and one she shares with them, is that the adoptive parents will change their minds. Our need to be assured that we will not be rejected is basic to our natures. We need that strong witness in our spirits, that we belong, that we are secure, that we are loved.

 Why do you think our adoption into God's family diminishes fear? How will that truth help you next time you are worried about something?

_____

_____

_____

"For I consider that the sufferings of this present time are not worthy to be compared with the glory that is to be revealed to us."

Romans 8:18

📖 Read Romans 8:17–18 and Hebrews 5:8. What is the maturation process Paul describes in these verses? Why must we suffer? What does it lead to? How does understanding this help us to persevere?

_____

_____

_____

_____

Our union with Christ is a package deal. Romans 6:5 tells us we share in His death and resurrection—both the negative and the positive. Christians who do not suffer with Christ need to question whether or not they are truly Christians. These verses and others like it explain that suffering is a necessary ingredient in the maturing process. Rather than doubting His love for us when He allows suffering in our lives, we can rejoice that He finds us worthy to share both in His pain and glory.

 In what ways has your suffering in the past enabled you to mature in your faith?

_____

_____

_____

 Read Romans 8:18–25. Why are the pains of childbirth an apt illustration of the way we persevere?

_____

_____

_____

I was just kidding when my first child was three weeks late and I said, "Maybe I am not pregnant after all; I think I'll just give up on the idea of having this baby." The "fruit" was obvious. I knew for sure, one way or another, a new life would eventually be born. And when the contractions finally started, I knew it would be relatively soon. In the same way, the fruit of God's work in our lives is obvious. We have a sure expectancy that He will complete the work He has begun. And the pain we go through will be worth it all when our "new life" is given to us in the resurrection.

APPLY How does the fact that creation is eagerly awaiting the redemption of your body increase your determination to partake of divine perseverance?

_____

_____

_____

PERSEVERING TO THE END

The following is taken from the *New Geneva Study Bible*:

> In declaring the eternal security of God's people, it is perhaps clearer to speak of their preservation than, as is usually done, of their perseverance [because] the reason that believers persevere in faith and obedience is not the strength of their own commitment, but that Jesus Christ through the Holy Spirit preserves them.[2]

This point is important to remember as we think about perseverance. In these last verses of Romans 8, Paul emphasizes that our future security rests in God's love, not in our ability to persevere. Remember we are simply partaking of His nature of perseverance, not somehow coming up with it on our own.

 APPLY What does it mean to you that Jesus Christ through the Spirit is *preserving* you? What are some of the ways He does that?

_____

_____

_____

📖 Read Romans 8:26–27. How does the Spirit help us persevere?

_____

_____

Paul has just said that if we hope for what we don't see, we eagerly wait for it with perseverance. Now, he says, in the same way the Spirit perseveres in His prayers for us. When we don't know what or how to pray, He continues to pray for us. We see, also, the Trinity's interdependence in these verses. Both the Son and the Spirit carry out the will of the Father, and they both intercede for us. Christ searches our hearts, knows the mind of the Spirit, and obeys the will of the Father. He is the great mediator. The three of Them work together to comfort, provide for, and encourage us. We can persevere because They faithfully persevere.

APPLY Can you recall a time when you were sure the Holy Spirit interceded for you _"with groanings too deep for words"_? How did that help you persevere?

_____

_____

_____

📖 Read Romans 8:28–30. How can we be so sure everything is going to work together for good? How does Paul define the _"good"_ he refers to in verse 28? How does God's sovereignty give us courage to hope?

_____

_____

_____

As we said in answer to the previous question, all three persons of the Trinity work together to bring us into conformity with Christ's image. That is the _"good"_ They are after. We may think we know what is good for us, but we need to realize that God's plan and purposes are higher than our own. What He ordains for us at the present moment is not the complete picture. Verse 30 lays out the whole process, and our strong hope is that He can and will bring it to completion.

Extra Mile
TRUSTING IN TRIALS

Compare Isaiah 50:4–10 with Romans 8:31–39. Think about how Satan brought trials and suffering to Isaiah, the Israelites, and Christ Himself, and then compare similar trials you face. God gives love and help to all His people, and we all must learn to rely on Him.

APPLY Can you remember a time when something happened that you did not think was "good" but God made it work out for good? Share it with your community.

_____

_____

_____

_____

📖 Read Romans 8:31–39. What reasons for perseverance are given in these verses?

_____

_____

_____

Paul's three questions: *Who is against us? Who will bring a charge against us?* and *Who can separate us from God's love?* address our major fears and reasons to give up hope. We fear the enemy is too strong, or our own sins are too pervasive, or Christ's love is not enough for us. Yet when we bank on the truth of these verses, we can conquer our fears and add up all the reasons to partake of the gift of perseverance.

APPLY Which of Paul's three questions trouble you most? Why?

_____

_____

_____

📖 Read Acts 14:19–22. How did Paul learn to persevere? How did he encourage the disciples he made? What do you think he meant by his statement at the end of verse 22?

_____

_____

_____

_____

We need to do in our own communities what Paul and Barnabas did in Lystra, Iconium, and Antioch. Our souls need strengthening, and we need to be encouraged to continue in our faith, for we face the same situation that every disciple has faced since the beginning of the church. We all must enter the kingdom of God through many tribulations.

APPLY In what ways can we strengthen each other's souls? What kind of tribulations have you had to face? How did they prove to push you further into the kingdom?

_____

_____

_____

_____

PERSEVERING IN COMMUNITY

An Old Testament story about persevering in community tells about God's people fighting together against Amalek (Exodus 17:8–16). Some were chosen for battle and others for intercession. Everyone needed the support of others around them, and they all needed God's support and grace in order to persevere. The battle with Amalek is a symbol of our battle against *"the corruption that is in the world"* (2 Peter 1:4). Like the Israelites, each of us must know and daily remind ourselves of our part in the battle because our situations and callings can change. And in order for the community to win in the battle, we all must know our callings and do our parts.

> **"After they had preached the gospel to that city and had made many disciples, they returned to Lystra and to Iconium and to Antioch, strengthening the souls of the disciples, encouraging them to continue in the faith."**
>
> **Acts 14:21–22**

Perseverance

Put Yourself in Their Shoes
EXODUS 17

As you meditate on Exodus 17, try to identify your calling today.

Are you one of the warriors in battle?

Are you called to intercession like Moses?

Are you called to a supporting role for others like Aaron and Hur?

📖 Read Romans 1:9–12. How did Paul partake of divine perseverance in relation to the Romans? How is that a model for our community relationships?

_____

_____

_____

Think of how much closer our communities would be if everyone followed this model of caring: unceasing prayer for each other; asking the Father to give us more opportunities to be together; longing to share our gifts with one another; and wanting to be encouraged by our corporate faith.

APPLY Have you ever had someone willing to be in unceasing prayer for you? How did that affect you?

_____

_____

_____

How would you rate yourself in unceasing prayer for each one in your community; asking the Father to give more opportunities to be together; longing to share your gifts with others; and wanting to be encouraged by corporate faith?

_____

_____

_____

📖 Read Romans 12:1–2 and 5. What new applications of this verse come to your mind when you consider the use and meaning of the word _body_ or _bodies_ in these verses?

_____

_____

_____

Marva Dawn in her book _Truly the Community_ makes the following observations:

> Paul urges the Romans to present their _"bodies"_ as _"a sacrifice, living, holy, and pleasing to God."_ He thereby exhorts them to deepen their unity by offering their various small bodies, or parts of the Church, as one whole, living, and holy sacrifice to God. In giving to God all of their respective groups, they would be drawn together by their service and worship into a more cohesive whole.[3]

This would definitely lead to more unity in the larger body of Christ. By sacrificing our denominational distinctives and pride, we could enjoy the fellowship of other believers and please God by our love for one another.

My church recently asked its members to sacrifice their comfort and connections by splitting the church in half in order to plant two new churches. The two new bodies are now able to more effectively serve two separate

Did You Know?

PAUL'S MODEL FOR COMMUNITY RELATIONS

■ Unceasing prayer for each one in your community

■ Asking the Father to give more opportunities to be together

■ Longing to share your gifts with others

■ Wanting and expecting to be encouraged by the faith of others communities. In a similar way small groups are often asked to divide in order to multiply. When we do so we are offering our *bodies* as sacrifices in order to serve and worship God as He desires and to take the gospel into more homes and reach more people for Christ. We are thereby persevering in the work of the gospel.

APPLY In what ways are you willing to sacrifice your "bodies" if the sacrifice Paul is referring to actually applies to the communities in which you are involved?

_____

_____

_____

Read Romans 12:3–8. How should we relate to others in the body of Christ? Where might perseverance be needed?

_____

_____

_____

We may find it difficult to use all the gifts God gives us among proud and controlling people. But if we persevere in humility and interdependence, we will allow people to use their gifts freely so they can grow in grace and in the exercise of their faith. Those who think highly of their own opinions rarely wait to hear and learn from others. They often fail to see value in other's gifts. Leaders who do not allow their members to exercise their gifts are cutting off arms or legs that God intended to help serve the body.

APPLY Why is the success of the community tied to your obedience in the role you have been given?

_____

_____

_____

Read Romans 12:9–13. What are some practical ways we can persevere in our love for one another?

_____

_____

_____

Paul gives twelve different ways to love each other in these verses. Your discussion should be rich in practical applications of each one. I want to comment on just two of them. In verse 11 he tells us not to lag behind in diligence. *Webster's Dictionary* says diligence means persevering application. This makes me think of 2 Peter 1:5, where we are told to "bring in all diligence" or to persevere in applying all the qualities of the divine nature in our shared faith. As we bring each gift into our midst and practice applying it to our relationships, we grow in our love for one another.

"Rejoicing in hope" (verse 12) is another intriguing phrase. I recently watched a movie called *The Pursuit of Happyness.* I was amazed at the main

character's perseverance. His secret seemed to have something to do with the way he rejoiced in hope. Personally, I got very frustrated and agitated when his life kept coming up against one tribulation after another. I thought I would have given up hope long before he did. Yet, as the father in the story kept telling his son to trust him, I realized that is what our heavenly Father tells us. We have far more reason to hope, and because of all Christ has done for us and promised us we can rejoice even in the midst of trials. Our times together should encourage just such responses to whatever happens.

📖 Read Romans 12:14–18. How do we persevere in our pursuit of peace and unity? Why is this so important to our community?

_____

_____

_____

Again, this passage is full of amazing directions for our lives together and for those relationships that are far more difficult. Overcoming evil with good is a monumental challenge.

Marva Dawn quotes one of the best explanations I have ever heard on the meaning of "*heap burning coals upon his head*" (verse 20, KJV). They suggest Paul quotes a proverb referring to an ancient Egyptian practice that both Hebrews and Romans would have understood.

> A penitent would go to the individual he had wronged, bearing on his head a clay dish containing burning coals. The meaning of the metaphor as it is used in proverbs then becomes clear: if a man acts generously towards his enemy he may bring him to repentance. And if this is the sense of the metaphor as Paul understood it, then he is telling us that if a Christian has an enemy, and instead of threatening him forgives him, then he is likely to bring his enemy to the point of repentance; metaphorically the Christian is himself putting the clay bowl of burning coals on the man's head and starting him on his way to repentance.[4]

Our pursuit of peace does not merely have goals of reconciling our relationships with others but their relationships with God as well. We want blessing, respect, joy, ultimate satisfaction, and renewal for all we meet. In seeking to bless others, we do all we can to bring them to peace with God. Starting them on their way to repentance is often a first step.

APPLY In what practical ways have you persevered in love and peace with others in your community?

_____

_____

_____

As I look back over this whole chapter on perseverance, it becomes apparent how vital prayer is in partaking of the divine nature. Please write your own prayer or join me in mine.

_____

_____

Our pursuit of peace does not merely have goals of reconciling our relationships with others but their relationships with God as well. In seeking to bless others, we do all we can to bring them to peace with God.

Father, we praise You for Your steadfastness, for Your forbearance, for Your longsuffering, for Your patience, for Your loving-kindness, and for Your faithful perseverance with us. You are so gracious and worthy of all our praise and thanksgiving.

Lord, we fall so short of this quality in our own strength. We are impatient, unfaithful, irritable, and independent. Please forgive us and enable us to stand firm in Your grace. Do what you need to in our hearts that grace might reign in us. Preserve us, O Lord, that we might persevere.

We pray that we may exult in our sufferings as we see them as a training ground for perseverance. Help us to believe the right things so we can live in resurrection power. Let us know that Christ's death conquered death and sin. Help us consider ourselves to be dead to sin and alive to God in Christ. May we live by grace, through faith every conscious hour.

Deliver us, O God, from the enemy's temptation to quit, or to despair, or to fear. Help us to identify his lies about how we don't need others, how we can make it on our own. Please give us Your vision for the body of Christ, Your grace to minister to one another, and Your boldness to reach the lost. May we heap coals upon the heads of all those who need repentance.

Works Cited

1. Lesslie Newbigin, *Sign of the Kingdom* (Grand Rapids, MI: Eerdmans, 1981), 69.

2. *The New Geneva Study Bible* (Nashville, TN: Thomas Nelson, 1995), 1781.

3. Marva Dawn, *Truly the Community* (Grand Rapids, MI: Eerdmans, 1992) 15.

4. Peter Cotterell and Max Turner, *Linguistics and Biblical Interpretation* (Downers Grove, IL: InterVarsity Press, 1989), 304.

Notes

7

Godliness

"**W**hat's the difference between godliness and righteousness?" I asked a group of seminary students who meet weekly with an older man they call "Captain." One of the students immediately said, "Righteousness is God's gift to us, godliness is how it is worked out in our lives." "I think he's right on!" said Captain.

This band of brothers speaks often about godliness. They also pray fervently for the church to return to a truer form of godliness. They grieve over the many lost souls in today's American churches who think they are saved because they walked down an aisle or said the sinner's prayer. But the failure to grow, the lack of fruit, and their ungodly lives makes an observer wonder if these folks really know the Lord and are truly saved.

My son, one of the brothers in this community, and I arrived late once when I visited the Captain's household. I will never forget the sight of men sprawled out in a star pattern in the middle of the living room floor. Face down, heads together, hands clasped with one another, they cried out to the Lord with tears, pleading for the lost, for the church, and for themselves.

At the close of the meeting, Captain gave me one of John Piper's books. He wrote on the first page, "Piper writes <u>nothing</u> new in these pages. The shame and wonder is that he labors so to merely

Captain's household . . .

a community of godliness

Word Study
GODLINESS

"Godliness is piety toward God and the proper conduct that springs from a right relationship with him. It is not the belief itself, but the devotion toward God and love toward man that result from that belief. . . . It is the sum total of religious character and actions. . . . It is not right action that is done from a sense of duty, but is the spontaneous virtue that comes from the indwelling Christ and reflects him."

Source: J. D. Douglas and Merrill Tenney, *New International Dictionary of the Bible* (Grand Rapids, MI: Zondervan, 1987) 342.

'recapture' sentiments that were once broadly embraced by most of God's Faithful. Must he be such a solitary source of light and heat for our age?"

The ten young seminarians in this community of godliness will one day be pastors spread across the world, not just on the Captain's floor. One just recently left to minister in Haiti. As they continue to diligently supply godliness in their shared faith, they will be additional sources of light and heat in God's kingdom.

Godliness

DAY ONE

2 PETER 1:3–7

*"Seeing that His divine power has granted to us everything we need for life and godliness through the true knowledge of Him who called us. . . . that you might become partakers of the divine nature. . . . For this reason bringing in with diligence supply in the faith of y'all the excellence and in excellence the knowledge and in knowledge the self-control and in self-control the perseverance and in perseverance the **godliness** and in **godliness** the brotherly kindness and in brotherly kindness the love."*

(Author's Composite Translation)

GODLINESS IN CHRIST

The word *eusebeia*, or godliness, is not found in any of Paul's letters to communities of the early church. He only used the word in letters he wrote to the young pastors, Timothy and Titus. Likewise, Peter also rarely used the word. He mentioned it in a sermon in Acts 3:12 and only four times in his epistles, three of those times in our passage (2 Peter 1: 3, 6–7). In verse 3 Peter tells us we find all we need for godliness (*eusebeia*) in our true knowledge of Christ. Then, verses 6 and 7 teach that *eusebeia* is one of the gifts we supply in our shared faith. Because it is so rarely mentioned, and the times Paul and Peter use it seem somewhat mysterious, we must be prayerful and careful in our study and discussion of godliness.

Today we will focus on one verse that not only teaches us of the godliness of Christ but also introduces us to the mystery of godliness. By the end of this chapter, I hope you will realize that godliness is far more than wearing a bracelet that reminds us to ask the question "What would Jesus do?" and then try our best to do it. Rather, it is the Trinity's mysterious interaction for us, within us, and among us that transforms our hearts, our minds, our actions, and our community.

📖 Read 1 Timothy 3:16. Why do you suppose Paul describes Christ as the great mystery of godliness?

_____

_____

_____

These verses seem strange at first glance. You would expect Paul to say how we should conduct ourselves in explaining the mystery of godliness. Yet he only writes of Christ. I believe Paul defines godliness by his description of Christ because godliness can be obtained only by faith in Christ and union with Him. Those who think that they can become godly by their own efforts to be like Christ fail to see the mystery.

📖 Read 1 Timothy 3:16; 2 Corinthians 3:18; 4:4–6. How do these verses in Corinthians help us understand the point Paul made to Timothy? In what way was Christ's *"appearing in a body"*(NIV) a revelation of godliness? How does that lead to our godliness?

_____

_____

_____

_____

_____

The possibility of godliness for us began when Christ came to earth and revealed the glory of God to those who truly saw Him—both as divine and human. In the book Captain gave me, John Piper compares and contrasts Christ's two natures with the following phrases:

"glory mingled with humility"
"transcendence accompanied by condescension"
"justice tempered with mercy"
"majesty in meekness"
"worthy of all good accompanied by patience to suffer evil"
"sovereign dominion clothed with a spirit of obedience and submission"[1]

Because Christ partook of our nature, He made it possible for us to partake of His. We can partake of the divine nature by receiving His Spirit. The Spirit enables us to see the glory of God in the face of Christ, and as we see we are mysteriously transformed into His image.

APPLY In your personal experience, how have you partaken of the divine nature? What evidence shows you are being changed from glory to glory?

_____

_____

_____

Read Mark 1:10–11; Romans 1:4; 1 Timothy 3:16 and 1 John 5:7, 9–11. When was and is Christ *vindicated <u>by</u> the Spirit,"* (NASB option), and what do you think that has to do with His godliness and with our godliness?

_____

_____

_____

At Christ's baptism, both the Father and the Spirit vindicated Him by visual and auditory expressions of their love and unity. Then by raising Christ from the dead, the Spirit of holiness declared Him to be the Son of God. Finally, the Spirit testifies for Him and thereby vindicates Him in our hearts. John Calvin explains it this way:

The testimony of the Spirit is more excellent than all reason. For as God alone is a fit witness of himself in his Word, so also the Word will not find acceptance in men's hearts before it is sealed by the inward testimony of the Spirit. The same Spirit therefore who has spoken through the mouths of the prophets must penetrate into our hearts to persuade us that they faithfully proclaimed what had been divinely commanded.[2]

The Holy Spirit proclaims Christ to be the Son of God, the second person of the Trinity. When we, by faith and by the Spirit's work in our hearts, are

Extra Mile

ANGELS, NATIONS, AND GLORY

Think about the final descriptions of the mystery of godliness in verse 16. When the angels beheld God being born as a baby, they proclaimed glory to God in the highest *and on earth.* Godliness was now on earth again. The angels first saw this mystery, and then as Christ grew to be a man and walked among us, many believed it. When He was taken up into glory, He sat down at the right hand of God and now intercedes for His brothers and sisters that they, too, may partake of godliness. The proclamation of His godliness among the nations brings them to their knees before His throne. And because this great mystery is revealed to the church, we can partake of godliness by faith in our union with Him.

united with Christ, we partake of godliness and are more and more changed into His image.

APPLY How do you expect the Holy Spirit to vindicate Christ as you read the Bible? Can you share a time when the testimony of the Holy Spirit made Christ more alive to you?

_____

_____

_____

_____

Read 1 Timothy 3:14–16. How does all of this help us to know how to conduct ourselves in the household of God? If, corporately, we are the pillar and support of the truth, how does the godliness of our lives affect the proclamation of truth?

_____

_____

_____

_____

This is the key point to grasp in this lesson. The church of the living God partakes of the godliness of Christ in our union with Him, lives out the mystery of godliness in our conduct toward one another, and supports the truth of godliness in our common confession. What we do and say and how we live in the household of God is all based on who Christ is. And the proclamation of who He is will draw others into God's household and see them partake of godliness, as well.

APPLY How would you describe *"the mystery of godliness"* after studying this lesson?

_____

_____

_____

Why is it important that we focus on Christ when we think and talk of godliness?

_____

_____

_____

How would you describe the difference between trying to be like Christ and actually partaking of His godliness?

_____

_____

_____

TRAINING IN GODLINESS

God has a way of keeping us on our toes. Just when we think we have things figured out, He seems to enjoy challenging our systems and conclusions. We are tempted to skip those verses that don't seem to line up with our doctrines, but we need to remember that all Scripture is true and worthy of our study. We may not be able to understand how two things are true when they seem to contradict each other, but we have to admit that God is higher, and some of His ways are past finding out.

The passages on godliness we will study today contain truth that may leave some of us with troubling questions. But that is okay. It is good to be humbled before the greatness of our God. We sought to establish that we grow in community, but we will see today that sometimes we grow alone. We have learned that God saves His chosen children, but will see today He desires all people to be saved. We have read and studied the truth that God grants everything we need for life and godliness and we are merely receivers, but we will see today we do have responsibilities. May God give us the grace to embrace the mystery.

📖 Read 1 Timothy 1:12–17. How does Paul describe his salvation in these verses? What factors are involved? To whom does he give all the credit?

_____

_____

_____

Did you notice how Paul describes himself in a passive, receiving manner? He not only gives Christ all the credit for his salvation, but he also describes himself as the chief of sinners. Christ strengthens him, puts him into service, shows him mercy, gives abundant grace, saves sinners, and demonstrates His perfect patience. Christ is the King, eternal, immortal, invisible, the only God, and so deserves all the honor and glory forever.

APPLY How would you describe your salvation? In what ways does it look like Paul's?

_____

_____

_____

_____

📖 Read Galatians 1:11–12 and 15–18. Why do you suppose Paul mentions that his initial training was in Arabia? Why do you think the Spirit sent him back to Damascus for three years after his desert experience?

_____

_____

_____

_____

Christ strengthens Paul, puts him into service, shows him mercy, gives abundant grace, saves sinners, and demonstrates His perfect patience. Christ is the King, eternal, immortal, invisible, the only God, and so deserves all the honor and glory forever.

We have no information about his training in Arabia except this one statement, but I think it implies that his time there was with Christ alone. Even though we are attempting to show how important the community is in our training, this passage describes something different. Mike Mason comments:

> The plain fact is, if you follow Jesus there will be times when you will find yourself absolutely alone, cut off from everyone. In spite of the glorious unity and love that are ours in the Body of Christ, there are bound to come times when the soul must stand utterly alone before God. For there are some traits of soul, some spiritual qualities, that can only be acquired and perfected in . . . the grueling solitary confinement of real loneliness and desertion. There is just no way around it. Without tasting this experience no Christian can become fully Christlike.[3]

But then, after his time in Arabia, Paul returned to Damascus and the community where a body of believers first embraced him. It is interesting to me that he spent three years with them before meeting any major church leaders. I think we can learn from this that we can grow and mature as Christians wherever God places us.

APPLY Describe a time in your Christian life and growth when you were absolutely alone? What was God doing in your life at that time?

_____

_____

_____

📖 Read 1 Timothy 2:1–5. What does prayer have to do with godliness?

_____

_____

_____

When we discussed these verses in one of my study groups, someone commented on verse 4, "So much for predestination." Just because God desires all people to be saved and asks us to pray for them, this does not erase the truth of predestination. Other verses make that doctrine clear. But these verses make our responsibility to pray clear. No one can ever adequately resolve the tension between the two truths of God's sovereignty and human responsibility. We simply and humbly need to accept both as true. And we should not overemphasize one over the other.

Those who emphasize God's sovereignty may wonder why He asks us to pray. These verses, and many others, indicate a real correlation between our prayers and the life we seek. God doesn't promise us anything that He does not ask us to pray for. Praying opens us up to receive, and is one means by which we receive all His good gifts.

We have emphasized the fact that God gives us what we need to grow in godliness, and supplies the gifts as we are together. But these verses call us to responsibility, as well. He gives us grants, but we have responsibility. Furthermore, we need to pray together, but also alone, in our prayer closets.

APPLY Theoretically, what position of priority does prayer hold for you? How does that work out in actuality? How can we encourage one another in this?

_____

_____

_____

📖 Read 1 Timothy 4:7–10. What do you think it means to *"discipline yourself for godliness"*? What are some practices mentioned in these verses that could be part of an exercise regime? In what way is godliness *"profitable for all things"*?

_____

_____

_____

_____

I believe we are to *"labor and strive"* not in a legalistic way, trying to "add to our faith" but rather striving to put ourselves in a position to receive what the living God would grant to us. Our hope is in Him, not in what we can achieve. Our labor is to bring forth what He has implanted within us.

On the other hand, the disciplines of being nourished by the Word, prayer, and the study of sound doctrine are all profitable and do train us in godliness. Paul's reference to bodily discipline sets an example that clearly indicates that we should exert disciplined effort in our spiritual training.

APPLY How does biblical training in godliness differ from what hypocritical liars might suggest?

_____

_____

_____

📖 Read 1 Timothy 4:11–16. How do you think godliness is taught to others?

_____

_____

_____

Prescription, teaching, exampling, public reading of Scripture, exhortation, exercising spiritual gifts, and perseverance are all ways that we learn godliness from one another. These are primarily done in community, not on our own. We need to take pains with all these things and be absorbed in them. It will take faith, excellence, knowing God and each other, Spirit-control, and perseverance (2 Peter 1:5–6). It will take time together. How this will *"ensure salvation both for yourself and for those who hear you"* is again a bit of a mystery for those who believe only God ensures our salvation. But there you have it. Maybe He provides it, but we ensure it. Or maybe, we just embrace the mystery.

Extra Mile
DOCTRINES OF DEMONS

Read 1 Timothy 4:1–6. When it comes to the area of discipline for godliness, there are many *"deceitful spirits and doctrines of demons."* Some people may tell us we must follow all their rules and regulations, abstain from things God intends for us to enjoy, and believe the fables they conjure up. In contrast, Paul tells us we must sanctify all things *"by means of the word of God and prayer"* and be *"constantly nourished on the words of the faith."* We are to *"follow sound doctrine"* rather than waste our time with fables the enemy feeds us or hypocritical liars who say they have obtained godliness through their self efforts.

APPLY Why do you think most of the disciplines Paul lists seem to take place when the body of Christ is gathered together?

_____

_____

_____

How could we use our time together in better ways to accomplish a mutual discipline of receiving God's grants?

_____

_____

_____

Godliness

"Likewise, I want women to adorn themselves with proper clothing, modestly and discreetly, not with braided hair and gold or pearls or costly garments, but rather by means of good works, as is proper for women making a claim to godliness."

I Timothy 2:9–10

GODLY WOMEN

The verses we are going to study today are among the most controversial verses in the Bible. They have been used over the years to put down women, and to bar them from meaningful ministry in the kingdom of God. Rather than entering into a controversy regarding women's roles in the church, let's focus on the sinful tendencies Paul says need to be addressed by women who desire to make a claim to godliness. In keeping with our goal to partake of the divine nature and build loving community, let's look at ways women need to repent and pursue godliness, and how men can support and encourage them.

📖 Read 1 Timothy 2:9–10. How does Paul contrast women who are godly with women who aren't? Do you think he is focusing on what they wear, what they do, or why they do what they do? What are the passions and desires behind these two opposing lifestyles?

_____

_____

_____

If Paul were simply prescribing a dress code in these verses, he would not tell the women to wear good works, instead, he would say wear dark colors, high collars, or bhurkas. Obviously, he is contrasting worldly women who dress for conquest and godly women who live for others. Our godliness will show on the outside by the way we dress, but it comes from within—hearts passionate to serve others, not ourselves.

 APPLY Why do you think some religions and churches demand dress codes for women? How would you describe a woman who wears good works?

_____

_____

_____

📖 Read 1 Timothy 2:11–14. What sinful tendencies are implied by Paul's directions regarding women in these verses? Why might quietness (rather than cleanliness) be next to godliness for women? Why is submissiveness important for a woman *"making a claim to godliness"*?

_____

_____

_____

_____

Just as Eve took over the conversation with the serpent, while Adam remained silent on the sidelines, women often use their verbal skills to dominate. We don't know exactly what was going on in Timothy's church at the time this letter was written. But, we can imagine the women getting carried away with their new liberty. They now could take part in the instruction that used to be reserved for men only and were given a voice they had not had before. I believe God calls women to submission and silence because our sinful desire to control and verbally dominate needs curbing.

APPLY As a man, what might a woman say or do that would indicate to you she had a controlling spirit? How would a godly woman be different?

_____

_____

_____

As a woman, how has God revealed to you your "need to control" as an ungodly trait? How has the discipline of submission helped you?

_____

_____

_____

📖 Read 1 Timothy 5:3–4, 9–10, and 16. Verse 4 tells the children and grandchildren of widows to learn to *"practice piety,"* or *eusebeo,* to their families. Although this is not the exact Greek word for godliness, it is very close. Why are relationships so important for those who make a claim to godliness? How does our care for one another validate our claim to godliness and relieve the burden of the church?

_____

_____

_____

_____

Loving and caring relationships are what our everyday Christian lives are all about. The description of a godly widow's life in verse 10 clearly illustrates that fact. We tend to measure godliness in a person's "spirituality," but Paul focuses on the way we treat one another, and specifically in this passage, the way we treat the elderly.

These instructions about the care of widows are much needed in our day. So many families are separated by many miles and, sadly in some cases, an even greater lack of concern and responsibility. Too many widows feel abandoned and lonely. Verse 16 puts a major responsibility on women to care for their aging parents. This is both a natural and spiritual responsibility. Few Christian women shirk their responsibilities to care for their children, but in our culture they often do not take the care of elderly parents seriously. I believe these verses tell us they should.

APPLY What are some things you can do to *"practice piety"* to older men and women in your family and community?

_____

_____

_____

📖 Read Titus 2:3–5. The phrase *"older women are to be reverent in their behavior"* can be literally translated "have lifestyles proper to priests." This is a fair description of godliness. How do the rest of Paul's verses further describe godly women? Why do younger women need such training? How can and should it be carried out within the community? How can men support this ministry?

_____

_____

_____

_____

Put Yourself In Their Shoes

TITUS 2

I wanted to title the Bible study I wrote on this passage *Women to Women,* but because the community model of discipleship was not yet popular, we settled on *Woman to Woman.* But I do believe more women would sign up for a ministry to younger women if it were a group effort, and if the men of the church eagerly supported it and did all they could to enable the women to have time together.

There has been a growing interest in how this mandate should be carried out in the church. Many younger women are seeking older women who would train them, yet are frustrated in their search. I believe there are several reasons why. First, women in our culture don't want to be considered "older." They fight against ever reaching that category. However, the word *older* is simply comparative. Everyone is older than someone, whether the disparity is measured in years or spiritual maturity. We all have something to give to those following us. But many older women hesitate to carry out this mandate because they fear the daunting responsibility of mentoring. I believe many churches have wrongly applied the world's concept of mentoring to this passage. Again, because of our culture's emphasis on individuality, we think only of one-on-one training. But as we have learned in this study, much of Scripture presents a community-based model of discipleship. Older women of the community can carry out the instruction in these verses best by working together to train all the younger women. As they bring their shared faith and various gifts to each other, searching the Scriptures together and praying for one another, the training is accomplished.

APPLY As a woman, what things in this lesson challenged you, and how are you going to pursue godliness in new ways?

_____

_____

_____

_____

As a man, how has this lesson helped you to understand the unique challenges women face, and how are you going to seek to help the women in your life?

_____

_____

_____

Distractions from the Pursuit of Godliness

Godliness is having the proper center. It puts Christ in the center, not self. But our flesh, the world, and Satan all provide many distractions to pull us off-center. Remember, in order to partake of the gift of Christ's godliness we need to stay focused on Him, spend time with Him and His body, devote ourselves to prayer and the study of His Word, and be constantly nourished by words of faith. Today we will study the sixth chapter of Paul's first letter to Timothy where he warns us about the many distractions we will need to overcome in order to continue our pursuit of godliness.

Read 1 Timothy 6:3–5. What popular doctrines in our day do not conform to godliness? In what ways do they not conform? According to these verses, what do they lead to, and why?

_____

_____

_____

Any doctrine that emphasizes self does not conform to godliness. Teachings of self-help, self-sufficiency, self-discipline, etc., are all suspect because they have the wrong center. As we saw in Day One of this lesson, the great mystery of godliness must begin and end with Christ. Other doctrines are so focused on *"controversial questions and disputes about words"* that they miss the central teachings of love and godliness. Another popular doctrine is "the health and wealth gospel" that teaches if we have the right kind of faith God will bless us with healing and material blessings, supposing godliness is a means of earthly gain. None of these doctrines agree with the sound words of Christ, and all lead to division, depravity, and confusion regarding the truth.

 Have you been in a church or community that experienced friction over doctrine or disputes about words? What was the outcome?

_____

_____

_____

"If anyone advocates a different doctrine, and does not agree with sound words, those of our Lord Jesus Christ, and with the doctrine conforming to godliness, he is conceited and understands nothing."

1 Timothy 6:3–4

Have you ever been taken in by a doctrine that did not conform to godliness? What happened?

_____

_____

_____

📖 Read 1 Timothy 6:6–11. Why does discontentment lead us away from godliness? What should be the ultimate basis of our contentment?

_____

_____

_____

"Earth has nothing I desire besides you. My flesh and my heart may fail, but God is the strength of my heart and my portion forever."

Psalm 73:25–26 (NIV)

One of Satan's favorite temptations is discontentment. It takes our eyes off Christ, and puts our focus on those things or relationships we think we need. In contrast, think of the words of the psalm printed in the sidebar. Only Christ can be the ultimate basis of our contentment.

Our culture in America is choked by the love of money, and few in the church have escaped its deadly grip. We need to seriously discuss how we can help one another flee from these things and pursue godliness and the other gifts Paul mentions in verse 11. (You may notice his list is quite similar to our list in 2 Peter 1.)

 Have you known others who have *"pierced themselves with many griefs"*? How did it happen? How was the church or community group able to help them?

_____

_____

_____

📖 Read 1 Timothy 6:12–16. Why do we need to *"fight the good fight of faith"*? What are we fighting against? What is the *"good confession"*?

_____

_____

_____

I believe Paul is calling us to fight against all the distractions that lead us away from the pursuit of godliness. Since it is a fight of faith, it calls us to a concerted effort to supply in our shared faith all the nourishment, gifts, grants, promises, and qualities God wants to give us as we partake of His divine nature together.

The good confession Paul mentions in verses 12 and 13 is summed up in Christ's words to Pilate in John 18:36–37, that His kingdom is not of this world, yet He is the King of kings and the Truth of all truth, and those who hear His voice partake of His truth and His kingdom. Or, we could look back to 1 Timothy 3:16 to find the *"common confession"* Paul makes there of who Christ is. Both of these confessions help us to take our focus off our present circumstances and ourselves and put it where it needs to be—on

Christ and His kingdom. Indeed, it carries Paul into a grand proclamation of praise to Christ in verses 15 and 16.

 Try to think of an example of someone who fought the good fight well. Then share this example with your community.

_____

_____

_____

📖 Read 1 Timothy 6:17–19. With what particular temptation do the rich have to contend? How does misplaced security distract us from the pursuit of godliness? How do we *"take hold of that which is life indeed"*?

_____

_____

_____

We should not think these words only apply to millionaires or billionaires of today. Everyone in America is rich when compared to the majority of people throughout the world or most people of history. Since we are so tempted to pride and conceit, we often fix our hope on our savings rather than God. One way to measure if our hope is in God or in riches is to consider the test Christ gave the rich young ruler in Luke 18:22. How much do we give to the poor? What is the extent of our generosity? Are we storing our treasure for the future in savings accounts or in heaven?

Throughout 1 Timothy 6, Paul seems to contrast two ways of life. One is the pursuit of happiness that grabs hold of pride, gain, and earthly riches. The other is a pursuit of godliness that grabs hold of faith, truth, contentment, and that which is life indeed—Christ Himself.

 What are some ways you are going to *"take hold of that which is life indeed"*? How can your community help you in that?

_____

_____

_____

"Jesus answered, 'My kingdom is not of this world. . . . You say correctly that I am a king. For this I have been born, and for this I have come into the world, to bear witness to the truth. Everyone who is of the truth hears My voice.'"

John 18:36–37

LIVING IN TRUTH AND GODLINESS

Godliness

DAY FIVE

Godliness includes a deep-felt desire for beloved community. When we have the right attitude toward God and others, we are drawn into community. When we don't, we are repelled from it. Our self-centeredness isolates us. But living in the truth with one another leads to more godliness because it requires us to be open and vulnerable. When we are honest about our sins and temptations, others can encourage us to repent and be cleansed. Truth and godliness produce a life worth living. Today we are going to study what Paul wrote concerning true godliness in his second letter to Timothy and in another letter that he wrote to Titus.

📖 Read 2 Timothy 3:1–12. What do you think Paul means by a form of godliness that denies its power? How does he contrast those he describes in the beginning of the chapter with those in verse 12?

_____

_____

_____

Someone once said, "Satan can imitate the gifts of the Spirit, but not the fruit." I think the power of godliness is similar to the fruit of the Spirit. Paul compares people in the church who outwardly may look as if they have God's Spirit working in them, but the fruit of their work proves they do not really know God, nor are they living by His power. Both Satan and the natural man are capable of pulling off some things that may look like godliness, but when persecution comes they will fall away. One of the blessings of persecution is its validation of true godliness.

🛑 APPLY Have you ever lived a form of godliness that denied its power? What was going on in your life at that time?

_____

_____

_____

📖 Read 2 Timothy 2:15–17 and 3:14–17. How does ignorance of God's Word and empty chatter lead to ungodliness? Why is it so important that we continue in the Word?

_____

_____

_____

The Word is truth. Empty chatter is what we come up with when we aren't continuing in the Word. When Paul says this kind of talk spreads like gangrene, he is implying that it can be deadly. We don't usually have such a negative view of our empty chatter. How much time do we spend in conversations that don't lead anywhere and have no redeeming value? In contrast, Paul holds up the Scripture as something that will give us wisdom and lead to salvation. It alone is inspired by God and is profitable for training in righteousness or godliness.

🛑 APPLY What happens in your life and in your small group when you are not focused on the Word of God?

_____

_____

_____

📖 Read Titus 1:1. How does godliness affect our knowledge of the truth or vice versa?

_____

_____

_____

_____

This verse, as translated by the New American Standard Bible, says the knowledge of the truth is according to godliness. In other words, we can't understand or enjoy truth without lives of godliness. If we say we believe the truth but live ungodly lives, chances are we do not really know the truth. Truth always teaches, reproves, corrects, and trains us to be righteous. The New International Version translation of this verse says the knowledge of the truth leads to godliness.

📖 Read Titus 2:11–14. How do we live godly (*eusebos*) lives according to these verses? How is that contrasted to ungodliness (*asebeia*)?

_____

_____

_____

Grace is the key word in this passage. Grace changes everything. It trains us to renounce ungodliness. Seth Anderson, a young man I met in seminary, preached that we should think of this training as boot camp. It is preparation for an important battle and necessary for our survival. The training changes us from lazy gluttons to fit servants or soldiers in God's kingdom. He pointed out that renouncing ungodliness was like rejecting with violence, similar to the way his wife screams "Off!" as she bats away a spider on her shoulder. He added that the same word is used in chapter 1, verse 16. There Paul warns Titus about so-called believers in Crete who profess to know God, but deny (or renounce) Him by their works.

Seth went on to say that God's grace works through people. He shared how his accountability to another man strengthened his own ability to renounce ungodliness. Saying no to ungodliness includes the little things. We need to get serious about the temptations Satan puts before us, saying, "This doesn't really matter. It is such a little thing. It won't affect your testimony, or your community, or your walk with the Lord. You can do it." Or "It doesn't matter if you don't do the thing the Holy Spirit is prompting you to do." Satan twists the meaning of grace and makes it a way to overlook our sin, rather than what it is—the power God gives us to not sin and to choose to do His will.

 In what ways does grace change everything for you?

_____

_____

_____

How does the idea of "rejecting with violence" help you with the ungodliness you are tempted to? How can others in your community help you reject ungodliness?

_____

_____

_____

"Paul, a bond-servant of God, and an apostle of Jesus Christ, for the faith of those chosen of God and the knowledge of the truth which is according to godliness."

Titus 1:1

Satan twists the meaning of grace and makes it a way to overlook our sin, rather than what it is—the power God gives us to not sin and to choose to do His will.

Concerted prayer is one means of partaking of godliness together. Pray earnestly with and for one another.

Our Father, who art in heaven, please hear our prayers and transform us into Your likeness. We praise You for the mystery of godliness. Thank You that You have made a way for us to share in Your Son's righteousness. We depend upon Your Spirit's work in us; only His fruit can make us godly. So we praise You, our triune God for this gift of godliness. May we revel in its generosity, and seek to unwrap and marvel at its many facets.

Lord, we confess our ungodliness. We are often content to remain in our natural state of sinfulness. We, as women hold on to control, thinking it is our security. We, as men, have not led with servants' hearts or provided for our families in ways that have met their every need. We have all focused on ourselves and our own selfish needs. We have not cared for our brothers and sisters or sacrificed for them, like You have sacrificed for us. Please forgive us, cleanse us, and renew our hearts.

We pray You would make us a holy priesthood built together into a spiritual house. Teach us what it means to be priests to one another. Strengthen us to be built together. Please knit our hearts together and open our homes and schedules to make more room for one another. May the spiritual house You are building have many guest rooms. May we be open and inviting to the lost souls around us. May our house be a house of prayer, a house of training, a house of healing, a house for all nations, and above all a house of love.

We pray that we would not be distracted by the enemy of our souls. Please deliver us from his temptations and enable us to stand firm in our resolve to partake of Your nature.

Deliver us from teachings of self-help, self-sufficiency, and self-discipline. Help us to focus on You and Your grace and enable us to depend more on each other. Help us to grab hold of that which is life indeed: Christ Himself and His body, the church.

Write your own prayer below.

_____

_____

_____

_____

_____

_____

_____

_____

Works Cited

1. John Piper, *God is the Gospel* (Wheaton, IL: Crossway Books, 2005), 52.

2. John Calvin, *Institutes of the Christian Religion,* 2 vols., ed. John T. McNeill, trans. Ford Lewis Battles (Philadelphia: Westminster Press, 1960), 79 (I.vii,4).

3. Mike Mason, *The Gospel According to Job* (Wheaton, IL: Crossway Books, 1994), 46.

8

Brotherly Kindness

lmost thirty years ago, Jerry and Hilda Stone stepped out in faith to buy a 5,200-square-foot home in the historic district of Raleigh, North Carolina. They believed God called them to offer housing and discipleship to single adults. The beautiful turn-of-the-century home was gently refurbished in the same way that lives would be refurbished by the brotherly kindness that is the essence of life at The Watered Garden. The Stones now believe every church should consider community housing for those without families or those who have never been affirmed or nurtured.

Matt, who lived at The Watered Garden, compared his experience there to the blossoming of a rose. "A bud already has the essential nature of a rose, but it takes the right environment (a watered garden) to encourage the unfurling that will manifest its goodness and fragrance. Likewise, a Christian has the divine nature within, but it takes a community to bring out the reflections of Christ's presence." We all need nurture, care, warmth, and watering to grow. Those who live in relational deserts have little hope for healthy growth.

Another resident suggested that brotherly kindness was an antidote to worthlessness. For years she saw herself as worthless, full of shame and self-loathing. Her own family did little to build her up—but much to tear her down. Living together with brothers and sisters in Christ and experiencing steadfast kindness from both genders brought healing to her wounded heart.

The Watered Garden

...a community of brotherly kindness

 **Word Study**
BROTHERLY KINDNESS (PHILADELPHIA)

Phil is from the root word *phileo* which means tender affection and respect.

Adelphia comes from the root word *adelphos,* which denotes a brother, a near kinsman, or, in the plural, a community based on identity of origin or life.

Source: *Vine's Expository Dictionary of Old and New Testament Words,* 1:154

This kindness is based on the fact that we are brothers and sisters, either in the greater sense of humanity, or in the more particular family of God. Brotherly kindness is opening our hearts, lives, and homes to all our brothers and sisters in an effort to show kindness, acceptance, generosity, and longing for relationship.

Acceptance and openness gives each person who lives at The Watered Garden the opportunity to find safety, honesty, sharpening, mutual edification, and love in a caring community.

THE BROTHERLY KINDNESS OF CHRIST

In order to partake of the divine nature of kindness, we first need to see God's kindness revealed in His Son. There is a natural family resemblance between God and Christ. Partaking of this nature involves becoming part of His family. Christ, as our elder brother, not only shows us the way, but His Spirit gives us hearts that long to care for our brothers and sisters as He does.

📖 Read Isaiah 30:18; 1 Thessalonians 1:6; 2:14, 17–20 and Revelations 3:20. What is God's motive for kindness? For what is Christ longing? Describe Paul's relationship with the Thessalonians. How was his longing similar to Jesus'? How are we to imitate Paul in this?

_____

_____

_____

_____

_____

Try to picture God the Father longing to be gracious and compassionate to us and Christ the Son patiently waiting for us to commune with Him. Then in the opposite realm, imagine Satan trying to keep us away from that communion and from being with the community of faith. For example, think of all the ways he tried to hinder you from coming to your discussion group.

Paul was *"eager, with great desire"* to see the Thessalonians and to be with them. Their spiritual growth and his hope to see them standing in the Lord's presence was his glory and joy. Can we say the same about our brothers and sisters? Do we care that much? Twice already Paul urged the Thessalonians to imitate him and other Judean communities. God calls us to partake of His nature of kindness so we can minister kindness to our brothers and sisters.

APPLY What particular ways of showing brotherly kindness come to your mind as you meditate on the way God the Father, Christ, and Paul showed loving-kindness? How do you envision them practiced in your community?

_____

_____

_____

📖 Read 2 Thessalonians 2:16–17 and Hebrews 13:1, 5–8. How do these verses describe Christ's brotherly kindness? Why do we need comfort,

2 PETER 1:3–7

*"Seeing that His divine power has granted to us everything we need for life and godliness through the true knowledge of Him who called us. . . . that you might become partakers of the divine nature. . . . For this reason bringing in with diligence supply in the faith of y'all the excellence and in excellence the knowledge and in knowledge the self-control and in self-control the perseverance and in perseverance the godliness and in godliness the **brotherly kindness** and in **brotherly kindness** the love."*

(Author's Composite Translation)

hope, and strength? What does the fact that Jesus is unchanging do for us?

_____

_____

_____

Again, we see in these verses the divine nature of kindness. The sight of it strengthens our heart to *"every good work and word"* of brotherly kindness. In the Hebrews passage, the writer tells us to *"let love of the brethren continue."* This phrase is translated from the same Greek word we are studying: *philadelphia.* After making a point to describe particular ways of showing brotherly kindness, the writer explains how and why we can show it: by focusing on God's faithfulness and Christ's trustworthiness. Because God's love endures forever, we can love our brothers and sisters. His love is the source of our love; His care is the source of our care; His help is the source of our help. His mercy is the source of our mercy. We are to become partakers of His nature. Notice also, we should imitate the faith of our leaders—another good reason to spend enough time together so we can observe faith in action.

APPLY How did God's mercy and goodness (an apt description of the divine nature of kindness) affect John Stocker's heart? What similar feelings have you experienced

_____

_____

_____

📖 Read Romans 15:1–6 and 2 Thessalonians 3:3–5. What is the opposite of brotherly kindness? Why do we need perseverance and godliness before we can partake of brotherly kindness? What do you think it means to be *"of the same mind with one another according to Christ Jesus"*?

_____

_____

_____

From the description of Christ in this passage in Romans we learn that He did not live to please Himself. The implication is that He did what we are called to do in verse 2. He lived to please His neighbors for our good and for our edification—because we are His neighbors, His brothers and sisters. And all He did for us was for our good and our edification. His mindset is to be our mindset. That is another way to think about partaking of His nature. When we partake of His nature of kindness, we cease to live only to please ourselves and become focused on what we can do for others' good and edification.

We need both perseverance and encouragement to make such dramatic changes in our priorities. Brotherly kindness is not an easy thing; in fact, it is impossible without God's gifts of perseverance and encouragement. Romans 15:4 tells us that Scripture gives us perseverance and encouragement. Then in 2 Thessalonians 3:5, we read that we obey His commands when our hearts are directed *"into the love of God and into the steadfastness of Christ."* These two Scripture passages together describe what we need to do in order to partake of God's nature of kindness: to persevere in our study of

"Your mercy is more than a match for my heart, Which wonders to feel its own hardness depart, Dissolved by Your goodness, I fall to the ground And weep to the praise of the mercy I've found."

—**John Stocker, 1776**

the Scriptures and to receive what He longs to impart to us. Our obedience will come from changed minds and hearts, not just our concentrated efforts.

 APPLY How effective has trying hard to obey been for you? Why do we resist the idea that mind and heart change must come first?

_____

_____

_____

📖 Read Romans 15:7. What does acceptance have to do with brotherly kindness?

_____

_____

This final note from Paul gets at the core of brotherly kindness. Author and pastor Jerry Cook writes about acceptance saying:

> There's no other way [than unreserved acceptance] to get close enough to people to help them at the level of their deepest needs. When we cultivate the habit of accepting people, they open up to us, they like us, they trust us instinctively. . . . Because we are accepted in the Beloved, we must be accepting of the beloved.[1]

It is important to understand the difference between our culture's definition of acceptance and what Paul means here. (See the word study pertaining to this in the sidebar). This is not the kind of acceptance that holds to no standard of conduct and makes no differentiation between good and bad. If we truly want to please our neighbors for their good and edification we will set our standards according to the Bible and will seek to edify or build them up to those standards. But before we can get to that, we need to welcome them into our midst and show special interest in each person. And if they are believers, we are to welcome them as brothers and sisters in the faith.

APPLY How can we practice acceptance and still maintain biblical standards?

_____

_____

_____

Word Study
ACCEPTANCE

In Romans 15:7, the word *"acceptance"* comes from the Greek *proslambano,* and literally means "to take to oneself or to receive, always in the Middle Voice, signifying a special interest on the part of the receiver, suggesting a welcome." (Source: *Vines Complete Expository Dictionary of Old and New Testament Words*, 3:255)

This same word is used in Acts 28:2 where Paul describes the extraordinary kindness of the natives of Malta, who *"because of the rain that had set in and because of the cold, they kindled a fire and **received** us all."* (emphasis added).

Brotherly Kindness

DAY TWO

GENTLENESS, TENDERNESS, AND FOND AFFECTION

In Lesson One we suggested that the qualities listed in 2 Peter 1:5–7 were not only a description of the divine nature, but were also gifts or grants from God. We receive these gifts by partaking of His nature. Also, each gift is found in the preceding gift, so it follows that by the time we partake of brotherly kindness we already have some degree of faith, excellence, knowledge, self-control, perseverance, and godliness. Today we will look more closely at the Thessalonian believers and discover not only their amazing growth in faith, but also how this occurred. From that we can see how it could happen in our own communities as well.

📖 Read 1 Thessalonians 1:1. Who wrote this letter? What implications concerning community do you find in that?

_____

_____

_____

Paul was not a lone ranger. He traveled, ministered, and even wrote with his brothers in Christ.

📖 Read 1 Thessalonians 1:2–10. How do the authors of this letter describe the Thessalonians? What evidence do you see that theirs was a community of faith, excellence, knowledge, self-control, perseverance and godliness?

_____

_____

_____

Paul's commendation of their *"work of faith"* implies both faith and excellence in its work. A *"labor of love"* indicates a measure of self-control in that what we do for others usually follows a denial of selfish desires. *"Steadfastness of hope"* and waiting *"for His Son"* imply perseverance. *"Knowing His choice of you,"* *"imitators of us and of the Lord,"* and turning *"from idols to serve a living and true God"* all indicate both a knowledge of Christ and partaking of godliness.

📖 Read 1 Thessalonians 2:3–9. What characteristics of brotherly kindness did Paul, Silvanus, and Timothy live out before the Thessalonians? How can we imitate them like the Thessalonians did? What do you think it means to *"impart not only the gospel of God but also our own lives"* to one another?

_____

_____

_____

_____

With their fallen natures, leaders and teachers often come into a community with exhortation tainted by error, impurity, manipulation, people-pleasing, flattery, and greed. We have all seen it many times, and to some degree expect it. However, these three men saw themselves as family. Rather than asserting the authority of apostles, they treated the Thessalonians as fragile children with gentleness and tenderness. Comparing themselves to nursing mothers gives us an amazing picture of brotherly kindness. The fond affection described in verse 8 points to deeply personal relationships.

> **"But we proved to be gentle among you, as a nursing mother tenderly cares for her own children. Having thus a fond affection for you, we were well-pleased to impart to you ... our own lives."**
>
> **I Thessalonians 2:7–8**

As visiting apostles, they did not stand apart and expect royal treatment, but evidently entered into work and honest labor with the Thessalonians. Isn't it true our hearts are often knit together as we work side by side? Our lives are imparted to one another not just in words spoken, but also in meals eaten together, in work accomplished together, and in fun enjoyed together.

Recently I watched a documentary about the Amish people. I was intrigued to learn that the decisions they make about what "worldly attractions" they allow are based on how they might interfere with community. The reason they drive horse-drawn buggies rather than automobiles is that cars make it easier to escape community. The Amish have discovered and established a way to impart their lives to one another, and I wonder if we should imitate some of what they do.

APPLY Which characteristics of brotherly kindness are most difficult for you personally?

_____

_____

_____

How do our difficulties make us aware that we need more of God?

_____

_____

_____

📖 Read 1 Thessalonians 2:10–13. In verse 11, what three ways of behaving toward the Thessalonians are mentioned? Why do you think it would be important that we include all three in our ministries as well?

_____

_____

_____

The New American Standard Bible (NASB) translates these three ways as *exhorting, encouraging, and imploring.* The New International Version (NIV) says *encouraging, comforting, and urging.* The first word in the Greek is *parakaleo,* and it means "to come alongside in order to call." The second word is *paramutheomai,* and it means to come alongside in order to comfort or encourage. The third word means to "implore or charge," and here the writers implore them to *walk* in a manner worthy of God. All three are pictures of walking together. We are to walk alongside our brothers and sisters through whatever life brings and whatever God calls us to in His kingdom. The three words are followed by the phrase, *"each one of you as a father would his own children."* Again we get the family image that is also in our phrase *"brotherly kindness"* and a personal application to each brother or sister.

APPLY How are you imparting your own life to the people in your community? What changes do you think the Spirit is calling you to make?

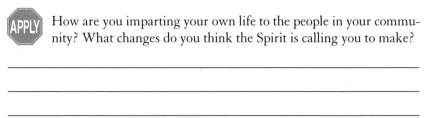

_____

_____

_____

Put Yourself in Their Shoes
IMITATION OF CHRIST

As an introvert, I enjoy writing alone. My challenge is that what I write about works best in community. Several years ago, a comment from someone in my community stopped me short. I was wondering why not many women in our church were interested in studying the workbooks I had written. "They don't want your books when they have you!" she said. I wanted to give them my words, but not my own life. For me, the first is far easier than the second. The women of my church want me to come alongside like Paul and his brothers did. They want brotherly kindness not just words on a page.

Come to think of it, this is similar to what God has done. In the Old Testament God sent prophets and gave written words to His people. But what is even more wonderful, in the New Testament, He sent His Son to come alongside us, and His Spirit to encourage and comfort us. And now He calls us to come alongside our brothers and sisters in kindness to imitate what He has done for us.

BUILDING UP VS. DESTROYING COMMUNITY

Chapters 3 and 4 of 1 Thessalonians not only describe the brotherly kindness Paul had for this community, but also contain dire warnings regarding what can destroy a community. As you study these verses keep in mind the contrast between building up and destroying. What specific things are involved with each? And how does a focus on community, as opposed to individuality, lead to each result?

📖 Read 1 Thessalonians 3:1–10. How many times do you see the phrase *"your faith"* in this passage? Is Paul referring to what they believe or how they believe? How do you think we *"complete what is lacking"* in the faith of others? What specific things did Paul do to complete what was lacking in the faith of the Thessalonians?

_____

_____

_____

_____

Some of Paul's statements in this passage would make me think he was rather codependent if he said such things in our culture. His personal happiness seems too tied to what they do, and his longing to be with them is repeated so many times it borders on overkill. Stop and think a moment of how much our culture changes the way we view relationships and limits our sense of responsibility for others.

Paul's desire to strengthen and encourage their faith indicates that he wants to help them live out the faith they have. His fear that Satan would tempt them to lose their faith points to how fragile faith can be. We all need others to help build up our faith *"until we all attain to the unity of the faith, and of the knowledge of the Son of God"* (Ephesians 4:13). How many of us can say with Paul that we *"really live"* when we see others stand firm in the Lord? Do we even care that much about the faith of others?

Paul was willing to endure persecution, send his right-hand man, pray most earnestly night and day, write encouraging letters, and long to be with his brothers. My own attempts at brotherly kindness fall far short of this.

APPLY How much of your time and effort is spent on building up the faith of your brothers or sisters? Do you think only some are called to that?

_____

_____

_____

📖 Read 1 Thessalonians 3:11–13. In Paul's prayer, what does he imply about the source of brotherly kindness?

_____

_____

_____

"For now we really live, if you stand firm in the Lord. For what thanks can we render to God for you in return for all the joy with which we rejoice before our God on your account, as we night and day keep praying most earnestly that we may see your face, and may complete what is lacking in your faith?"

I Thessalonians 3:8–10

Consider the following words of Charles Spurgeon.

> Divisions are our disgrace, our weakness, our hindrance. As the gentle Spirit alone can prevent or heal these divisions by giving us real loving fellowship with God and with one another, how dependent we are upon Him for it. Let us daily cry to Him to work in us brotherly love and all the sweet graces that make us one with Christ, that we all may be one even as the Father is one with the Son, that the world may know that God has indeed sent Jesus and that we are His people.[2]

Many spiritual directors teach we should pray the prayers of Scripture more often. If we would, like Paul, pray earnestly night and day that God would direct our ways to one another and cause us to increase and abound in our love for one another, He would establish our hearts unblamable in holiness. Rather than just trying in our own strength to be kind to one another, we should earnestly pray for His kindness to flow through us. By partaking of His nature we are taken into a much deeper ocean of grace, generosity, and kindness for our brothers and sisters.

 How often do you pray that God would direct your way to others and cause your love to abound for them? Does your community need to rethink your most common prayers for one another?

_____

_____

_____

Read 1 Thessalonians 4:1–8. How does Paul contrast defrauding the brethren with true brotherly kindness? How does sexual immorality destroy community?

_____

_____

_____

When we remember the stories of David and Bathsheba, King Arthur in Camelot, or the Trojan Wars, we see how immorality destroys community. But why is immorality so destructive to community? I believe that's because sex is an image of intimacy. Community is built on commitment, and commitment is fed by intimacy. But false intimacy destroys both commitment and community. Think of Paul's image of the church as living stones built together for a holy priesthood. The mortar that holds us together is healthy connections. But throw in sexual immorality, and the mortar turns to sand, and the brotherhood is defrauded or destroyed.

 Share stories from your own life experiences of how community was either built up or destroyed.

_____

_____

_____

Read 1 Thessalonians 4:9–12. Why did the Thessalonians have *"no need for anyone to write"* to them about brotherly kindness? What do you

"Do you not know that your bodies are members of Christ? Shall I then take away the members of Christ and make them members of a prostitute? May it never be!"

1 Corinthians 6:15

think is Paul's point about leading *"a quiet life"* and attending *"to your own business"*? Is he now advocating isolation?

_____

_____

_____

One night, after working on this lesson all day, I watched the 2004 movie *Crash*. I would not recommend this movie as entertainment, but it does chronicle what happens when a culture is stripped of brotherly kindness. I am afraid that many in the church today have not been *"taught by God to love one another"* but have been taught by the world to hate, fear, bolt our doors, and build walls of self-protection. We need people like Paul to write to us about brotherly kindness to offset what our culture has taught us. Our world says: "Every man for himself, and don't trust anyone!" Bigotry, racial hatred, greed, fear, power, and lack of communication have replaced generosity, kindness, commitment, and faithfulness.

I believe Paul's words in verse 11 do not lead us away from community but rather explain how we should use the resources gained by work to bless and enrich our communities. Deuteronomy 24:20 promises the Lord will bless the work of our hands if we are generous to outsiders, just as 1 Thessalonians 4:12 states we will not be in any need ourselves when we practice brotherly kindness coupled with honest work.

APPLY What specific ideas for building up your community do you want to practice as a result of this lesson?

_____

_____

_____

CARING FOR THE COMMUNITY

I n the final chapter of his first letter to the Thessalonians, Paul gives specific instructions in how they are to care for the community. What he says would have been easily understood and accepted in the culture of that day but is more difficult in the context of our culture. Since the Enlightenment period of the eighteenth century, Western thought has focused on the individual. We think and act based on how things will affect us, our families, and our close friends. To overcome this misunderstanding, try to read our verses today with the following truth in mind: all the "one another" phrases in Paul's letters could also be translated as "yourselves together."

📖 Read 1 Thessalonians 5:11 and Hebrews 10:24–25. How would you describe encouraging and building others up? What were the Thessalonians and Hebrews doing?

_____

_____

_____

Word Study
EDIFY

Oikodomeo is a combination of two words, *oikos*, which means family, home, circle of friends, or community; and *domeo*, which means to build. This is quite different than how we think of building up someone's self-esteem, or clarifying an individual's understanding of a particular doctrine. Paul is talking about building up an *oikos* or community. The author to the Hebrews wants us to consider how we can stimulate the community to build itself up in love. That is why we can't forsake our assembling together. Encouragement and building up happen organically in a community of brotherly kindness.

In their helpful book *Encouragement: The Key to Caring*, authors Larry Crabb and Dan Allender ask the important question, "What can we do to shift our attention back to relating to God and to each other in loving fellowship and mutual ministry?" Their answer is similar to what we are discovering in this study. They conclude that all church activities should be "consciously and continuously regarded as means for drawing us closer to God and making disciples of all."[3] The following quotes give some of their definitions of encouragement.

> Encouragement is careful selection of words that are intended to influence another person meaningfully, toward increased godliness . . . to stir up, to provoke, to incite people in a given direction. Verbal encouragement includes the idea of one person's joining someone else on a journey and speaking words that encourage the traveler to keep pressing on despite obstacles and fatigue. . . . Encouragement depends on loving motivation in the encourager as well as wisdom to discern the needs of the other person accurately. The actual words may be admonishing, rebuking, correcting, reproving, instructing, explaining, sympathizing, reflecting, affirming, or self-disclosing. If the motive is love and the target is fear, the words will be encouraging.[4]

APPLY How does the translation "yourselves together" change your understanding of the "one another" passages?

_____

_____

_____

How does your community build up "yourselves together"?

_____

_____

Read 1 Thessalonians 5:12–13. What does brotherly kindness toward our leaders look like?

_____

_____

_____

In my years of church ministry, I have worked under seven different pastors. I remember many sad stories of unkind parishioners who did not esteem their pastors highly in love. Satan used these people, who may have thought they had good reasons to do what they did, to not only wound the leader's hearts but in many cases to bring disunity or destruction to the church. Leaders are always prime targets for the enemy. If he can bring them down in the minds and hearts of the people, he can spread discontent and rumors. Living at peace with one another and with our leaders is more important than being right, getting our way, or any number of excuses we might have to cause discord. Appreciation and loving respect are nonnegotiable. Since God gives authority to our leaders, we must honor them.

 Think of examples you know or have heard of where Satan has caused discord by attacking leadership. Encourage yourselves together by quoting Scriptures that tell you how your community could resist him.

_____

_____

_____

📖 Read 1 Thessalonians 5:14–18. What instructions for caring for the community are given in these verses? How well do we do this?

_____

_____

_____

Here Paul gives instructions for dealing with difficult people. We can't just hope that such persons will go away or that someone else will minister to them. Rather, Paul urges us to meet them at their point of need and to offer brotherly kindness that will reflect God's love. We have found that a team approach works best with difficult cases. In this way, one person does not have to carry the whole load which often leads to burnout. Each person on the team can be responsible for a few specific things, ideally in the area of his or her giftedness. Together they can be sure the individual is growing and being honest with everyone involved. Times of prayer with everyone involved bring joy and thanksgiving as we see the body of Christ functioning under the direction of the Holy Spirit.

APPLY What approach do you take in dealing with difficult or extremely troubled people? Would a team approach help? How would you facilitate that?

_____

_____

_____

📖 Read 1 Thessalonians 5:19–24. How do these instructions benefit community?

_____

_____

_____

 Extra Mile
HOLY KISS???

Read 1 Thessalonians 5:23–28. The Greek word for "kiss" in verse 26 is *phileo*, which is usually translated "brotherly kindness." What do you think may be inferred by *phileo* also meaning kiss? What else do Paul's words in these verses teach us about cultivating community? You can't escape the affection implied by the word kiss. Our care for one another must be genuine and rooted in our mutual love. Sometimes I wish we could be more expressive in our love for one another, and go beyond a friendly handshake. Even if kissing is only appropriate in certain cultures, I wonder if our love for one another would grow if we practiced more meaningful forms of expression.

These verses remind us that the Spirit wants to direct our efforts at brotherly kindness and speak into our lives and ministries. He works in our hearts and through the spoken and written word. As a community we are to stay open to His promptings, and to examine everything carefully. Together we can better discern His voice and His leading. We don't take a democratic approach to decision making, but as a community, we depend upon the Holy Spirit to guide us.

Paul's closing words in this letter to the community at Thessalonica again remind us that God sanctifies us, preserves us, brings our calling to completion, and gives us the grace of our Lord Jesus Christ. Paul's repeated request that we pray for one another implies that prayer is our part in bringing in the kingdom.

In what ways have you despised prophetic utterances? Why is it hard to hear the word of the Lord from someone else? How do we examine everything carefully?

_____

_____

_____

Who are the brothers and sisters in your *community of faith*? What new things has this lesson encouraged you do to build them up?

_____

_____

_____

Brotherly Kindness

> By partaking of His nature, by knowing we are in Him, by the amazing intimacy and unity we have with Him, He allows us to share in His glory. We are made beautiful by His glory in us. His name is glorified when we reflect His beauty.

TOUGH KINDNESS

In their second letter, Paul and his brothers continue to give thanks and praise for the Thessalonians' love and brotherly kindness. By saying they often speak proudly of them among the churches, they commend them for their faith and perseverance. This faith enables them to *"fulfill every desire for goodness"* even in the midst of persecution. But like many Christians with the gift of mercy, they need to be reminded that true brotherly kindness must, at times, be tough. Some among them were taking advantage of their generosity. True kindness to those who take but never give must be carefully redefined.

📖 Read 2 Thessalonians 1:11–12. What do you think it means to *"fulfill every desire for goodness"*? What is Paul's ultimate goal for the Thessalonians?

_____

_____

_____

The first thing to notice about these verses is they are a prayer. Everything God expects of us He tells us to pray for. We are not only to desire to do good for our brothers and sisters, but we are also to pray that God would fulfill those desires. Prayer is the means God wants us to use to become what He wants us to be. It is in and through prayer that we partake of His kindness, which then enables us to show kindness to others.

The name of our Lord Jesus should be glorified in us; when this happens, we are then glorified in Him. This is an amazing statement. Stop and think what this might mean. Majesty, beauty, and joy are all wrapped up in glory. As God's grace and power enables us to show goodness and kindness to others, we glorify His name. By partaking of His nature, by knowing we are in Him, by the amazing intimacy and unity we have with Him, He allows us to share in His glory. We are made beautiful by His glory in us. His name is glorified when we reflect His beauty.

APPLY How often do you pray for those in your community, that God would fulfill their desires to show kindness to others? How might you remind yourself to do it more often?

_____

_____

_____

📖 Read 2 Thessalonians 3:6–9. What kind of example did Paul set for the Thessalonians? Why do you think he needed to set that example?

_____

_____

_____

Whenever a community becomes known for its generosity and kindness, some will try to take advantage of it. Paul knew there would be those "users" who would expect the church to take care of them. But a careful scrutiny of their lives will show them to be unruly, undisciplined, and idle. It is okay and even necessary to set boundaries to protect ourselves and the church from this. If Paul had expected the Thessalonians to provide for them, even though they had a right to that expectation, it could have been a model others might use to take advantage of the church. Paul wanted to set a clear example of responsibility and hard work.

APPLY What boundaries have you set in your personal and community life? How can we help one another set and keep those boundaries?

_____

_____

_____

📖 Read 2 Thessalonians 3:10–12. When does kindness need to be tough?

_____

_____

_____

Paul identifies two types of people who need toughness: those who don't work and those who spend too much time in other people's business. A handout is not kindness towards those who refuse to work. That will merely enable their undisciplined lifestyle. They need exhortation and a command in the Lord that they must work. Kindness toward busybodies is an exhortation for them to eat their own bread and quit judging the freshness of someone else's.

📖 Read 2 Thessalonians 3:13–15. Why do you think Paul expects we might grow weary of doing good or showing brotherly kindness? What instructions does he give to deal with difficult people?

_____

_____

_____

Word Study
BUSYBODIES

Busybodies are those who waste their labor in "meddling with, or bustling about, other people's matters . . . some who are not busied in their own business, but are overbusied in that of others."

Source: *Vine's Expository Dictionary of Old and New Testament Words*

Marshall Shelley has written an interesting book entitled *Well-Intentioned Dragons: Ministering to Problem People in the Church.* The title alone captures one reason we burn out in ministry. The author points out that most "problem people" don't consider themselves difficult. They have good intentions and don't see themselves as busybodies. Because they are blind to what they are doing, they need loving confrontation or admonishment.

Not associating with certain persons is not the same as writing them off or cutting off all contact. Disassociation has an intentional goal of putting them to shame while still calling them brothers or sisters. We are tempted to think of them as enemies, but Paul reminds us they are brothers and sisters who need our loving-kindness, even if it is in the form of tough discipline.

APPLY Have you experienced a "well-intentioned dragon" at your church? What happened, and how was it handled?

_____

_____

_____

📖 Read 2 Thessalonians 3:16 and 18. Why do we need the Lord's peace, presence, and grace?

_____

_____

_____

Normally, showing brotherly kindness is a joy and fills our hearts with satisfaction. But when we are dealing with the kinds of situations Paul refers to in this letter we especially need the Lord's peace and grace. The confrontation and discipline he calls us to require His presence and step-by-step guidance.

Since prayer has proven to be a vital part of showing brotherly kindness, let's commit this lesson and what we have learned to God in prayer. Please write your own prayer in the space provided.

_____

_____

_____

_____

_____

_____

_____

_____

_____

_____

Our Father, we praise You for Your kindness to us. Thank You for making us Your sons and daughters, for bringing us into Your family. We love You, and long to be vessels of Your love to the world around us. We praise You that we are accepted in the Beloved, and that He is the same yesterday, today, and forever.

We confess that we are slow to partake of Your nature of brotherly kindness. We cling to our self-centered nature in hopes of realizing our own dreams and desires. We are often kind only when it somehow serves us. Rather than building love into our communities, we sometimes aid the enemy in bringing destruction to them by our selfishness, judgment, and prejudice. Please forgive us, and cleanse us.

We pray that You will direct our ways to one another and cause us to increase our love for one another, and establish our hearts unblamable in holiness. We pray for Your kindness to flow through us. Take us into Your deep ocean of grace so that we may overflow with generosity and kindness for each other. Please give us wisdom to know how best to care for our brothers and sisters, and boldness to show tough love when that is what they need.

Deliver us, we pray, from evil and all the temptations Satan would use to trip us up, or worse yet, to totally destroy our community. Please protect our community from his using any one of us as a fire-breathing dragon. We know that *"the tongue is a fire, the very world of iniquity."* It *"is set among our members as that which defiles the entire body, and sets on fire the course of our life, and is set on fire by hell"* (James 3:6). Please give us wisdom, caution, direction, and protection, for Your sake, and the sake of Your body here on earth. Fill us, we pray, with tender affection and gentleness.

Works Cited

1. Jerry Cook and Stanley C. Baldwin, *Love, Acceptance and Forgiveness: Equipping the Church to Be Truly Christian in a Non-Christian World* (Ventura, CA: Regal Books, 1979) 17–18.

2. Charles Spurgeon, *What the Holy Spirit Does in a Believer's Life* (Lynnwood, WA: Emerald Books, 1993) 41.

3. Larry Crabb and Dan B. Allender, *Encouragement: The Key to Caring* (Grand Rapids, MI: Zondervan, 1984) 12, 14.

4. Ibid., 20, 79.

Notes

9

Love

It was the spring of 1993. That summer our church was hosting a vacation Bible school and several leaders decided what they needed most was prayer. They didn't want to have the usual two-hour planning sessions that ended with ten minutes of prayer. They wanted to switch the priorities by spending most of their time in prayer and ending with a ten-minute business meeting. The results were phenomenal. Not only was the Bible school a huge success, but the prayer meetings continued and grew and are still meeting every week to this very day.

The community eventually became known as Women in Prayer. Since individuals have come and gone, the participants and leadership have changed over the years. But the things that remain constant are the reasons for the group's success and longevity. From the beginning, the focus was to enter into God's presence and to come before the throne of grace together. The women wanted more from God and were passionate in their desire to be transformed. As they shared their faith, God supplied all they needed for life and godliness.

The original group desired a great VBS ministry, but God's plan was to enter into every part of their lives and community and touch it with His excellence. The original focus was to learn to praise Him, but God's plan was to multiply grace and peace in a true knowledge of Christ. They determined to honestly confess their sins to one another every week, and God used that to supply

Women in Prayer

. . . a community of love

Love

DAY ONE

2 PETER 1:3–7

*"Seeing that His divine power has granted to us everything we need for life and godliness through the true knowledge of Him who called us. . . . that you might become partakers of the divine nature. . . . For this reason bringing in with diligence supply in the faith of y'all the excellence and in excellence the knowledge and in knowledge the self-control and in self-control the perseverance and in perseverance the godliness and in godliness the brotherly kindness and in brotherly kindness the **love**."*

(Author's Composite Translation)

self-control in their battle against the world, the flesh, and the devil. Week by week their perseverance grew, and month by month they saw new evidence of godliness in their lives. Over the years, many have benefited from the generosity, kindness, and care of these women. Several years ago, a single woman who was part of the group, received round-the-clock care in her final weeks of life. Because of the kindness of her sisters in Christ, she was able to stay in her own home and die with dignity.

Over the years the women in this community have partaken of all the aspects of the divine nature together. They have been blessed by receiving and practicing the grants and precious promises the Father has given us in Christ. But they all agree, the greatest gift of all was love. Relationships that were friendly at best became bonds that time, distance, and change will never break. One of the early participants said, "For those of us with small children, it was the highlight of our week. Most of us scheduled our lives around Women in Prayer. We learned the best way to develop close friendships is to go wholeheartedly into our devotion to God with others." Love increased and produced fruit in the true knowledge of our Lord Jesus Christ (2 Peter 1:8).

THE LOVE OF JESUS

Today we are going to study 1 Corinthians 13:4–7 by looking at Christ's love. In these four verses, Paul writes a description of love that Christ lived out. Christ did it perfectly, not only to fulfill the law of love but also to show us what His love will look like in us. As you think about your answers to the discussion questions, consider how Christ wants to change your heart to enable you to love as He loved.

Read 1 Corinthians 13:4 and John 13:1–5, 12–17. How did Jesus reveal patient, kind, and humble love?

_____

_____

_____

In John 13:14 Jesus explained why He washed His disciples' feet—so they would learn to wash one another's feet. I don't think Jesus was establishing a ritual. Rather, He was illustrating the patience, kindness, and humility that love takes in serving others. We need to look for a cultural equivalent to foot washing: something that needs to be done every day and usually given to the least important person to do, like washing dishes or taking out the trash. Nothing is too lowly if it needs to be done for the benefit of someone else. We were made in God's image to love and serve Him and others. The promised blessing that comes from loving and serving others in humility is the joy and satisfaction of fulfilling our purpose in life.

 What would enable your love to be more patient, kind, and humble? What can you do to see that happen?

_____

_____

📖 Read 1 Corinthians 13:5, Luke 23:34, and 1 John 3:16. How is Christ's death for us the greatest expression of love the world has ever seen? What are these verses calling us to?

_____

_____

_____

A prayer from *The Valley of Vision*, a compilation of Puritan prayers from the sixteenth century, clearly captures the love of Christ revealed in His death for us.

> Christ was all anguish that I might be all joy,
> Cast off that I might be brought in,
> Trodden down as an enemy
> That I might be welcomed as a friend,
> Surrendered to hell's worst
> That I might attain heaven's best,
> Stripped that I might be clothed,
> Wounded that I might be healed,
> Athirst that I might drink,
> Tormented that I might be comforted,
> Made a shame that I might inherit glory,
> Entered darkness that I might have eternal light.[1]

When Jesus tells us to deny ourselves and take up our crosses, He is calling us to sacrificial love. The love He showed on the cross displayed *agape*: my loss for your gain. Human love says, "I will do for you if you will do for me." But Christ gave us one-sided love, *"While we were yet sinners, Christ died for us"* (Romans 5:8). Many all around us in desperate straits have little to offer us, but need Christ's love. He calls the church as His arm of love to demonstrate compassion. People do not have to deserve or reciprocate our love. We offer it freely.

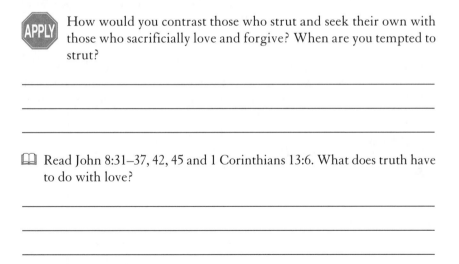

How would you contrast those who strut and seek their own with those who sacrificially love and forgive? When are you tempted to strut?

_____

_____

_____

📖 Read John 8:31–37, 42, 45 and 1 Corinthians 13:6. What does truth have to do with love?

_____

_____

_____

Extra Mile
LOVE DOESN'T STRUT

Read 1 Corinthians 13:5 and Luke 19:30–41. *The Message* paraphrases the first phrase in verse 5 as *"love doesn't strut,"* and Luke gives us a glimpse of such love. Those in Jerusalem were not looking for a loving Messiah; they wanted a strong, powerful leader who would deliver them from the Romans. They must have been confused by this humble man on a donkey, who wept over the city He loved. They were used to strutting leaders.

In his interaction with Jewish religious leaders, Jesus equated knowing truth with love. Love cannot exist where truth is rejected. He saw hatred and blindness proceeding from hearts embroiled in darkness and lies. In His love, Jesus became the truth that would set us free. He rejoices in truth, and so must we if we are to reflect His love.

What do you think it looks like to *rejoice in unrighteousness*? Remember and share a time when you rejoiced in the truth.

_____

_____

_____

_____

📖 Read John 21:12–17 and 1 Corinthians 13:7. How did Jesus' treatment of Peter after his denial illustrate a love that bears, believes, hopes, and endures all things?

_____

_____

_____

> *"Now may our Lord Jesus Christ Himself and God our Father, who has loved us and given us eternal comfort and good hope by grace, comfort and strengthen your hearts in every good work and word."*
>
> *2 Thessalonians 2:16–17*

Jesus' love for us must be coupled with His grace in order for Him to bear with us, believe in us, hope in us, and endure us. His grace is more than just His merciful forgiveness, it includes the power His gives us, enabling us to accomplish more than what is possible in our own sinful natures. We all see ourselves in Peter and know we deny Christ when we live out of our sinful natures. But Christ loves us, comforts us, and gives us good hope by grace. In other words, He can believe in us and hope in us because He gives us the grace to be faithful. His grace enables us to live in His life and love with His love.

Dick Woodward makes the following observation about Peter.

> Jesus gave a nickname to a man named Simon. Simon's life was a walking definition of instability. Yet Jesus called him "Peter," which means "rock" or "stability." Jesus called this man a rock for three years, even though he continued to be unstable during the three years he spent with Jesus. After Pentecost, Peter was the rock-like leader of the New Testament Church. People have a tendency to live up to what we call them.[2]

His point is a good one and reminds us that when we love others we also need to remember the power of the grace of God within them. Then we can call them to more than what is humanly possible, so they will depend upon God's grace.

What would help you to bear with and believe in your brothers and sisters more?

_____

_____

_____

_____

_____

_____

THE WAY TO FELLOWSHIP

W hat John wrote about Christ in his Gospel account is fleshed out in his first epistle as he describes how the body of Christ relates to one another. John opens his letter with a clear statement of how he experiences complete joy and fulfillment in this life. Enlightening truth surfaces when we look at John's letters with a focus on how we are to cultivate a loving community. He clearly teaches that loving one another is most important, and he shows us the way to find true fellowship. It is not a matter of trying hard to care more, or trying to stir up some positive emotions to feel more, or even trying to do more good deeds. Primarily, he wants us to be opened and cleansed vessels—so united with Christ we can partake of His love and allow it to flow through us to others.

📖 Read 1 John 1:1–4. What is John's goal in writing this letter? What basis for fellowship is implied in these verses? How was John's joy made complete? What do you think that means?

_____

_____

_____

_____

John wanted true fellowship or loving community and knew that it came about through sharing what we know of Christ with one another. When we proclaim to others what we have seen or heard of Christ we help to establish a foundation for true fellowship. Each of us has been given a measure of faith (Romans 12:3) to see and hear something of Christ. When we all bring our knowledge of Christ into the community, we help one another know Christ better, which leads to deeper fellowship with the Trinity and with one another.

Dan Allender has written an insightful book called *To Be Told*. In it he proves how important it is for us to tell our stories to one another. John points out in these verses that what we have heard and seen concerning the Word of life is the key thing to tell. As we share the truth, our fellowship is cultivated and our joy is made complete.

> God creates a story with each person's life, a story that we are meant to tell. And since we are called to tell our story, we are also called to listen to the stories of others. . . . God is calling us to fully explore, to fully enjoy, and to fully capture the power of the Great Story, the gospel. And we are to invite others to immerse themselves in the Great Story. One way we do this is by listening to our lesser stories and then telling them to others.[3]

 How often do you share with your brothers and sisters in your community what you have heard and seen of Christ in your walk with Him? Why might this be difficult?

_____

_____

_____

> *"What we have seen and heard we proclaim to you also, so that you too may have fellowship with us, and indeed our fellowship is with the Father, and with His Son Jesus Christ. These things we write, so that our joy may be made complete."*
>
> *1 John 1:3–4*

Where do you find joy? Why do you think it rarely seems complete? What are some things you could do to make it more complete?

_____

_____

_____

📖 Read 1 John 1:5–8. Compare and contrast walking in the darkness with walking in the light. What do those who walk in darkness say, according to verse 8?

_____

_____

_____

I used to think walking in darkness was what the heathen do, but John is writing to Christians and warning them about a kind of darkness they can fall into. I now believe this is a darkness of isolation and denial. It has to do with false fellowship, or the kind of surface relationships that have little basis in truth. It is a darkness that falls over churches where people wear their masks and pretend to love those they don't really know. Walking in the light is being honest about ourselves and our sins. It is establishing relationships based on complete honesty and trust in the power of the blood of Jesus.

Author David Augsburger writes in his book *Dissident Discipleship* about what he calls a tri-polar spirituality. He contrasts the kind of Christianity in the world today that is more about what God can do for me (or even what God and I can do together), with a tripolar spirituality that understands the importance of community.

> The person in community, the self in tripolar relationship with God and neighbor . . . joins fully with those who travel the path from one-dimensional narcissism through two-dimensional religiosity to a full, three-dimensional spirituality of radical participation in the multiple richness of actual, local, creative personal communities.[4]

To participate in this multiple richness, we must be honest with ourselves, with God, and with our neighbors. To join fully, we must be transparent and willing to forgive, even as Christ has forgiven us.

(APPLY) When and why are you tempted to walk in darkness? What lies does the enemy try to feed you?

_____

_____

_____

📖 Read 1 John 1:9–10. What must we do to find cleansing? What keeps us from doing it?

_____

_____

_____

We don't want to confess our sins because that is very hard on our pride. We are much more comfortable pretending we are good Christians who have everything together. Then we can live in a Pollyanna world where everything is going just fine. Our denial gets so polished that we don't even see we are claiming to be without sin. But there is no cleansing and no fellowship in a place like that. We must confess our sins to clear the way for God's love to flow through us.

In their book *Peace Making Women*, Tara Barthel and Judy Dabler explain what walking in the light means.

> To walk according to the light is to live perfectly, just as Jesus lives—something none of us can do. Walking in the light doesn't require perfect living, but it does require truthful living. It is a rich concept that includes, among other things, a penetrating honesty about our imperfection. Light dispels darkness, and walking in the light allows us to see and honestly acknowledge the truth about ourselves.

Similarly, Jesus contrasts doing evil with practicing truth in John 3:20–21. He teaches that those who do evil love the darkness, but those who practice or live in truth come to the light. He calls us to let the light of the truth expose our sin, which then should lead us to confession and repentance.

APPLY Have you ever been convicted of calling God a liar? What happened?

_____

_____

_____

📖 Review 1 John 1:1–10. What do these verses imply about love, both for God and for others?

_____

_____

_____

Love must be based in truth—not only the truth of the gospel, the truth of who Christ is, but also the truth about us. In real community we speak the truth to one another in love. Speaking the truth leads to fellowship, and fellowship makes our joy complete. This is true both in our relationships with one another and in our relationship to God. He knows us completely, forgives us completely, and loves us completely. The more we know and forgive others, the more we can truly love them.

THE LOVE OF GOD PERFECTED IN US

Love

My friend Christy Miller, the director of the Northwest Speaker's Bureau, posed a question well worth our consideration. She asked, "Since there is no punctuation in the Greek language, what if we put a colon rather than a comma after the word "love" in Galatians 5:22? It would explain why the word "fruit" is singular, and provides a great new resource for defining love. Each of the words following "love" could be a description of love's effects." The possibilities of this alternate interpretation intrigued me. Joy and peace could be the results of receiving God's love. Patience, kindness, and goodness would describe His love flowing through us to others. And faith, meekness, and self-denial could be how we return God's love to Him. This gives us a great picture from Paul of the love of God perfected in us. With this in mind, let's return to John's letter, and see what more he has to say about love.

📖 Read 1 John 2:1–6. In whom is the love of God being perfected? What do you think that means? Is our *keeping* and *walking* causes or effects of love?

_____

_____

_____

The love of God is being perfected or made complete in those who truly know Him. Christ, by His Spirit working in us, daily enables us to more and more love both God and others with His love. Our part is not to try to love more, but to seek to know Him more.

Although John talks about the keeping of God's commands and walking in the same manner as Christ walked, I don't believe he is telling us we must make every effort to do what Jesus would do. We are not merely trying to be like Him. John says we know we are in Him, and His love is in us, when we bear the fruit of His love.

By tying Paul's description of love with John's statement in this passage, we can say we have come to know Him when we have joy and peace in our hearts. We have come to know Him when we show patience, kindness, and goodness to those around us. We have come to know Him when His love enables us to respond to God with faith, meekness, and self-denial. John says if we abide in Him, we will automatically keep His commandments, love as He loved, and walk as He walked because we are bearing the fruit of His love being perfected in us.

APPLY In what ways have you seen God's love perfected in you?

_____

_____

What do you think of the idea of the fruit of the Spirit being love, and the other words in the list being descriptors of the effects of love?

_____

_____

_____

📖 Read 1 John 2:7–11. What is the new/old commandment John is writing about? What is new about it? What does light have to do with this command? What do you think John means by light and darkness?

_____

_____

_____

_____

I think John was remembering and commenting on the words Jesus spoke to him and the other disciples just before He went to the cross. They are printed in the sidebar.

If we go back to the first chapter of John's letter and remember what we discovered about light and darkness, it helps us to understand what John is saying here. The command to love one another is new in that it is now true in Him. Because it is true in Him, it can also be true in us. Don't miss that last statement, it is critical. Let me repeat it again. Loving one another is a "new commandment" because it is now possible to keep. It is true in Him and can be true in us. Because of His advocacy and propitiation for our sins, we can now walk in the light. We not only can be honest about our sins, but we can also love and forgive others who sin against us. Because of His Spirit dwelling in us and loving through us we can abide in the light and help one another find healing and avoid stumbling.

Because God's love is being perfected in us, we can love one another in ways that will help us all quit stumbling in the dark. We are now connected and can support each other. In our honesty about sin in our lives, we can challenge and confront one another in love. As we walk in the light together, we can live authentically with the kind of relationships that tell the world we are disciples of Christ.

 What proportion of the time would you say you live in darkness rather than light? How can you begin to change that?

_____

_____

_____

_____

📖 Read 1 John 2:15–17. What is the difference between _loving the world and the things in the world_ and loving God and our brothers and sisters? How does John define the "world"?

_____

_____

_____

We need to hear this important distinction in our materialistic culture. Since American society is so focused on the lust of the flesh, the lust of the eyes, and the pride of life, it often pulls us into its vortex. John juxtaposes the love of the Father with the love of the world, and thereby implies that receiving the Father's love, and letting it fill our hearts is how we can be set free from the love of the world. As the love of the Father is being perfected in us, our affections grow for Christ and for others, and they push out the lesser affections that take hold of our hearts. Saint Augustine understood this, and we would do well to pray his prayer quoted in the sidebar each time the love of the world tempts us.

"A new commandment I give to you, that you love one another, even as I have loved you, that you also love one another. By this all men will know that you are My disciples, if you have love for one another."

John 13:34–35

_"Come, Lord, work upon us
Set us on fire and clasp us close,
Be fragrant to us,
Draw us to Thy loveliness:
Let us love,
Let us run to Thee."_

Saint Augustine

APPLY In what ways does the love of the world tempt you most?

_____

_____

_____

📖 Read 1 John 3:11–19. How do we know *"we have passed out of death into life"*? What does that mean? What descriptions of love does John give in these verses?

_____

_____

_____

Abiding in death sounds so morbid, but John uses that phrase to describe people who have not been perfected in the love of God. Those who have not been lavished by His love still entertain thoughts of hatred and murder. We all need to move out of death into life, and when we do we are given a supernatural endowment of love. It is not just a one-time passage but needs to be made whenever we slip back into our worldly ways. Our part is to consciously and continually partake of the divine nature of love. Then we are to practice using His endowment of love.

Let's put together what John, Peter, and Paul teach us about love. John's description of love reminds me of the other qualities we have studied from 1 Peter 1:5–7: faith, excellence, knowledge, self-denial, perseverance, godliness, and brotherly kindness. Like the descriptors Paul gives to love in Galatians 5, Peter lists similar qualities that produce authentic love. Then John describes the life of love that is built by partaking of each quality of the divine nature. To love in deed and truth with abundant generosity and complete self-denial takes all the supernatural aid Christ offers.

 What things can you do that will enable you to know and love Christ more? How do you expect that will eventually change your relationships with others?

_____

_____

_____

Love

ABIDING IN LOVE

So far, we have studied Christ's love, the importance of honest vulnerability in love, and an introduction to how Christ's love is perfected in us. Today we continue to look at the mysterious truth that God wants to perfect His love by inviting us into the love of the Trinity to abide with Him there. Don't expect to fully understand this by the end of the lesson. But join me in exploring the possibilities John introduces in this amazing letter he wrote to his community and to us.

📖 Read 1 John 3:23–24. In what sense can believing and loving be commanded? Why is that more difficult for us than a command to some active deed? What various factors need to be in place before we can love one another?

_____

_____

_____

_____

We naturally think our choices to believe something and to love someone are individual rights. No one can tell us what to believe. No one can tell us who to love. We think our belief is a response to being convinced. Our love is a response to the way we are treated. Yet, here John tells us that God commands us to believe and to love. Saint Augustine once said, "Command what You will and give what You command." This is exactly what God does. He commands faith, but He also gives us the gift of faith. He commands love, but He also gives us the gift of the Holy Spirit to love through us. Our part is to receive His gifts, to partake of His nature, and then to practice using them in our day-to-day living.

John is not saying that obedience compels God to abide in us. Our obedience is an indication that He is abiding in us, enabling us to believe in His Son and to love others. Our abiding in Him, and He in us is reflecting and completing the communion of the Trinity. Our loving one another brings that communion into our daily living.

🛑 **APPLY** What is your initial response to the idea of being commanded to believe and to love?

_____

_____

_____

📖 Read 1 John 4:7–12. How and when is God's love manifested in us? What does it mean to *"live through Him"*?

_____

_____

_____

Imagine God's love as a gentle whirlpool, where the Father's love is mixed with the Son's love and the Spirit's love in a gentle swirl of joy and peace. Then they created us in their image to share their love, and we for a short time did abide in that love. But then we fell into sin, and God cast us out of the garden of love. Propitiation is Christ's work to overcome the effects of the fall. Propitiation is the cause that brings us back into loving relationship. John paints a picture here of God's love being made complete as we return to that place of abiding. His love is manifested in us by the propitiation of the Son drawing us back into the whirlpool of His love. We live through Him as we allow His love to flow through us to others.

"Beloved, let us love one another, for love is from God . . . If we love one another, God abides in us, and His love is perfected in us."

1 John 4:7, 12

Word Study

PERFECTED IN LOVE

First John 4:12 states that God's *"love is perfected in us."* The Greek word for perfected in this verse comes from the root word, *Teleios*, which means to end, or make complete, or finish the course. W. E. Vine says it is "to bring to an end by completing or accomplishing . . . the Father's will." Love is perfected or completed when all of God's children abide in the love of the Trinity and share it with one another.

Source: *Vine's Expository Dictionary of Old and New Testament Words*, III, 174

APPLY In what sense does Christ's propitiation apply to not only your relationship to God but also to the children of God? How is that worked out in the way you relate to others?

_____

_____

_____

📖 Read 1 John 4:13–16. What does it mean to abide in love? How do we do that? What efforts do we need to make?

_____

_____

_____

To abide is to remain stable or fixed in a state, so we are to continue or stay in a place of love. Being saved is being brought into the Trinity's life and love. Our part seems to be to know the Spirit within us, to behold the Son, and to acknowledge that He is the Son of the Father. When we do that, God mysteriously abides in us, and we abide in Him. In that way we come to know and believe the love God has for us. Abiding in love is abiding in God, and allowing God to abide in us.

It sounds so simple and straightforward, yet in our practical day-to-day living, it gets complicated. We still experience the effects of the Fall. We forget to listen to the still small voice within; we take our eyes off Christ, and our lips are silent when we have opportunities to confess God's love before others. We need to remind each other to abide in His love, and let it flow in us, around us, and through us. Because of the nature of love, it cannot be done alone. It must be tripolar: God, you, and me.

APPLY In what ways could others in your community help you to abide in love?

_____

_____

_____

📖 Read 1 John 4:17–21. What do you think John means when he says, "_As He is, so also are we in this world_"? In what way does perfect love cast out fear? What kind of fear is he talking about?

_____

_____

_____

_____

John's words remind me of what Paul wrote in Romans 8:1, 39. There Paul refers to the fear of condemnation or punishment. When we abide in the love of Christ, and know that we can never be separated from it, fear is banished. But John takes it a step further and explains that when we are perfected in God's love, we not only don't fear judgment, but we will also portray His love in this world by the way we love one another. If "_as He is_" refers to the love of the Trinity, what *we are* would be the completion of that love as His love flows through us to our brothers and sisters.

Tara Barthel and Judy Dabler relate the following about this verse:

> When we know God loves us, we lose our fear of the future and we find freedom. When we love God, we find hope. When we love our brother, we find peace. When our brother loves us, we find joy.[6]

APPLY Are you ever plagued by fear? How can today's lesson help you deal with that? How can your community help you deal with it?

_____

_____

_____

How do Charles Wesley's words in his famous hymn printed below help you to understand this lesson more clearly?

_____

_____

_____

Love Divine, All Loves Excelling
Love divine, all loves excelling,
Joy of heaven, to earth come down;
Fix in us Thy humble dwelling;
All Thy faithful mercies crown.
Jesus, Thou art all compassion,
Pure, unbounded love Thou art;
Visit us with Thy salvation;
Enter every trembling heart.

Breathe, O breathe Thy loving Spirit
Into every troubled breast!
Let us all in Thee inherit,
Let us find the promised rest;
Take away the love of sinning,
Alpha and Omega be;
End of faith, as its beginning,
Set our hearts at liberty.

Finish, then, Thy new creation,
Pure and spotless let us be;
Let us see Thy great salvation
Perfectly restored in Thee;
Changed from glory into glory,
Till in heaven we take our place,
Till we cast our crowns before Thee,
Lost in wonder, love, and praise.

—Charles Wesley, 1747

WALKING IN TRUTH AND IN LOVE

This is our final lesson and probably the most important. If we can grasp what it means to walk in truth and love and actually do it, everything we have studied up to this point will be fulfilled. The reason for partaking of faith, excellence, knowledge self-control, perseverance, godliness, and brotherly kindness is to enable us to walk in truth and love. We have seen that partaking is best done in the context of community and, of course, this walking, likewise, is done with our community. Walking in truth and love can only be done with others. We cannot do it alone.

📖 Read 1 John 5:1–3. Why does John equate loving God with loving the children of God and observing His commandments? To what commandments do you think he is referring?

_____

_____

_____

In Matthew 22 Jesus summarized all of the commandments of God into two: the greatest was to love God and the second to love our neighbors. John essentially says the same thing. Loving God, loving the children of God, and observing God's commandments all depend on love. Loving is not a burden; it is the fulfillment of our ultimate purpose. It is the exercise of all the gifts God has given; it is the practice of all the qualities He has granted to us; it is the result of partaking of His divine nature.

📖 Read 2 John 1–6. What is truth? What do you think it means to *"love in truth"*? What does John mean that the truth abides in us? What does it mean to walk in truth? How does that help us love one another?

_____

_____

_____

Word Study
TRUTH (ALETHEIA)

"In Greek literature, truth was intellectual. But in the Hebrew world, truth was more relational. It was defined as dependability, uprightness of character, and trustworthiness. John's use of the word in these verses can be interpreted to mean sincerity, integrity, and reality in the way we relate to God and to one another."

Source: *The New Bible Dictionary,* (Grand Rapids, MI: Wm. B. Eerdmans Publishing Co., 1973), 1301

The relational component of truth implied by John may seem strange to us because Greek philosophy has influenced our way of thinking. But let your mind and heart be transformed so you can see truth in a new light. In John's community truth was not just facts. Although truth could be known as fact, it was also something you love in, something you abide in, and something that abides in you. Remember, Jesus said He was the truth. If truth is a person, not just intellectual ideas, then how we live and walk in relation to that person defines our grasp of the truth.

I think loving in truth must refer to a type of love based on the truth of Christ: who He is, what He has done for us, and what He has called us to. It would also be based on the truth about us: who I am and who you are. This demands honesty and vulnerability. Furthermore, loving in truth will be dependable and trustworthy. If I love you in truth, I will be true to you. If truth is abiding in me and I am walking in truth, Christ's love will be evident in me.

APPLY How difficult is it for you to grasp the New Testament meaning of truth? Why?

_____

_____

_____

📖 Read 3 John 1–8. What is John's greatest joy? What do you think it means to *"accomplish something for the brethren"*? What does it mean to be *"fellow workers with the truth"*?

_____

_____

_____

To John, walking in truth and walking in love were the same thing. When he described his children walking in truth, he talked of the love they showed to strangers and to fellow workers with the truth. Walking in truth is acting faithfully towards the brethren. Mutual love, mutual support, and mutual prosperity add up to joy.

APPLY In what ways do you *"accomplish something for the brethren"*?

_____

_____

_____

📖 Imagine yourself as the chosen lady (2 John 1) or Gaius (3 John 1). How might John's words change you and transform the life of your community?

_____

_____

_____

It is wonderful how all of Scripture blends together and interprets itself by itself. John's words to the beloved members of his community can help us understand 2 Peter 1. As we discuss these words, our shared faith will strengthen and establish our love, bringing the kind of joy John felt into our own hearts and lives. You are loved just as much as the chosen lady or Gaius. Just as John sent his ancient letter to them, the Holy Spirit sends it to you. Receive Christ's love; partake of His nature, and then go out and spread it all around—to your spouse, to your children, to your church family, to strangers, to your fellow workers, to your community, to the world.

APPLY How and when do you feel the love of Christ most strongly? How is His love manifested in your life? What are you going to do to increase the probability that you will continue to walk in truth and love?

_____

_____

_____

_____

Receive Christ's love, partake of His nature, and then go out and spread it all around.

Closing Prayer:

Father, we praise You for Your love for us in sending Your Son. Christ, we praise You for the love You manifested both in Your life and death on our behalf. Holy Spirit we praise You for bringing God's love into our hearts and enabling us to love others with Your love.

Lord, we confess as we look at our lives and our walk before You that we still see so much selfishness and self-centeredness in our priorities. Please forgive us and cleanse us from this unrighteous living. Help us to walk in truth and love. May Your kingdom come and Your will be done in our lives.

Please give us grace to continue to pursue relationships with others who share our faith. Give us diligence to continue bringing in all of Your gifts and precious promises. Please enable us to supply in our shared faith the excellence of Your kingdom and to work together to spread it wherever we go. As we walk in Your excellence give us more and more knowledge of Your Son and fill us with Your Spirit. In that knowledge may we learn to let go of all our fleshly desires and yield control to Your Spirit. Please help us to persevere in yielding so we can partake of Your godliness. And in godliness may we show brotherly kindness to all we meet. We know now that all of this will bring us into Your love and enable us to express that love to one another and to everyone around us.

Deliver us, we pray, from evil in all its manifestations. Deliver us from our own efforts to be virtuous. Deliver us from knowledge that puffs up. Deliver us from our desire to control. Deliver us from fleshly endurance that is full of complaint. Deliver us from self-righteousness. Deliver us from insincere kindness. And deliver us from false love. Please enable us to walk in truth and love. For Thine is the kingdom, and the power, and the glory forever. Amen.

Write your own prayer below.

_____

_____

_____

_____

_____

_____

_____

Works Cited

1. Arthur C. Bennett, editor, *Valley of Vision: A Collection of Puritan Prayers and Devotions* (Carlisle, PA: The Banner of Truth Trust, 1989), 42.

2. Dick Woodward, "A Prescription for Love" (Hampton, VA: International Cooperating Ministries).

3. Dan B. Allender, *To Be Told* (Colorado Springs, CO: Waterbrook Press, 2005), 4.

4. David Augsburger, *Dissident Discipleship* (Grand Rapids, MI: Brazos Press, 2006), 80.

5. Tara Barthel and Judy Dabler, *Peace Making Women* (Grand Rapids MI: Baker Books, 2005), 215.

6. Ibid., 314.